LSAT Hacks

LSAT Preptest 72 Explanations

A Study Guide for LSAT 72
(June 2014 LSAT)

Graeme Blake

Blake Publications
Montreal, Canada

www.lsathacks.com

ISBN 13: 978-1-927997-07-9
ISBN 10: 1-927997-07-0

Testimonials

Self-study is my preferred way to prep, but I often felt myself missing a few questions each test. Especially for Logic Games, I wanted to see those key inferences which I just couldn't seem to spot on my own. That's where *LSAT Hacks* came in. These solutions have been a tremendous help for my prep, and in training myself to think the way an experienced test taker would.

- **Spencer B.**

Graeme paraphrases the question in plain terms, and walks through each step in obtaining the right answer in a very logical way. This book uses the same techniques as other guides, but its so much more consistent and concise! By the time you read through all the tests, you've gradually developed your eye for the questions. Using this book is a great way to test your mastery of techniques!

- **Sara L.**

Graeme's explanations have the most logical and understandable layout I've seen in an LSAT prep book. The explanations are straightforward and easy to understand, to the point where they make you smack your forehead and say 'of course!

- **Michelle V.**

"Graeme is someone who clearly demonstrates not only LSAT mastery, but the ability to explain it in a compelling manner. This book is an excellent addition to whatever arsenal you're amassing to tackle the LSAT."

- **J.Y. Ping, 7Sage LSAT,**
www.7Sage.com

I did not go through every single answer but rather used the explanations to see if they could explain why my answer was wrong and the other correct. I thought the breakdown of "Type", "Conclusion", "Reasoning" and "Analysis" was extremely useful in simplifying the question. As for quality of the explanations I'd give them a 10 out of 10.

- **Christian F.**

LSAT PrepTests come with answer keys, but it isn't sufficient to know whether or not you picked the credited choice to any given question. The key to making significant gains on this test is understanding the logic underlying the questions.

This is where Graeme's explanations really shine. You may wonder whether your reasoning for a specific question is sound. For the particularly challenging questions, you may be at a complete loss as to how they should be approached.

Having these questions explained by Graeme who scored a 177 on the test is akin to hiring an elite tutor at a fraction of the price. These straightforward explanations will help you improve your performance and, more fundamentally, enhance your overall grasp of the test content.

- **Morley Tatro, Cambridge LSAT,**
www.cambridgelsat.com

Through his conversational tone, helpful introductions, and general recommendations and tips, Graeme Blake has created an enormously helpful companion volume to *The Next Ten Actual Official LSATs*. He strikes a nice balance between providing the clarity and basic explanation of the questions that is needed for a beginner and describing the more complicated techniques that are necessary for a more advanced student.

Even though the subject matter can be quite dry, Graeme succeeds in making his explanations fun and lighthearted. This is crucial: studying for the LSAT is a daunting and arduous task. By injecting some humor and keeping a casual tone, the painful process of mastering the LSAT becomes a little less painful.

When you use *LSAT Hacks* in your studying, you will feel like you have a fun and knowledgeable tutor guiding you along the way.

- **Law Schuelke, LSAT Tutor,**
www.lawLSAT.com

Graeme's explanations are clear, concise and extremely helpful. They've seriously helped me increase my understanding of the LSAT material!

- Jason H.

Graeme's book brings a different view to demystifying the LSAT. The book not only explains the right and wrong answers, but teaches you how to read the reading comprehension and the logical reasoning questions. His technique to set up the games rule by rule help me not making any fatal mistakes in the set up. The strategies he teaches can be useful for someone starting as much as for someone wanting to perfect his strategies. Without his help my LSAT score would have been average, he brought my understanding of the LSAT and my score to a higher level even if english is not my mother tongue.

- Patrick Du.

This book is a must buy for any who are looking to pass or improve their LSAT, I highly recommend it.

- Patrick Da.

This book was really useful to help me understand the questions that I had more difficulty on. When I was not sure as to why the answer to a certain question was that one, the explanations helped me understand where and why I missed the right answer in the first place. I recommend this book to anyone who would like to better understand the mistakes they make.

- Pamela G.

Graeme's book is filled with thoughtful and helpful suggestions on how to strategize for the LSAT test. It is well-organized and provides concise explanations and is definitely a good companion for LSAT preparation.

- Lydia L.

The explanations are amazing, great job. I can hear your voice in my head as I read through the text.

- Shawn M.

LSAT Hacks, especially the logic games sections, was extremely helpful to my LSAT preparation.

The one downside to self study is that sometimes we do not know why we got a question wrong and thus find it hard to move forward. Graeme's book fixes that; it offers explanations and allows you to see where you went wrong. This is an extremely helpful tool and I'd recommend it to anybody that's looking for an additional study supplement.

- Joseph C.

Regardless of how well you're scoring on the LSAT, this book is very helpful. I used it for LR and RC. It breaks down and analyzes each question without the distraction of classification and complicated methods you'll find in some strategy books. Instead of using step-by-step procedures for each question, the analyses focus on using basic critical thinking skills and common sense that point your intuition in the right direction. Even for questions you're getting right, it still helps reinforce the correct thought process. A must-have companion for reviewing prep tests.

- Christine Y.

Take a thorough mastery of the test, an easygoing demeanor, and a genuine desire to help, and you've got a solid resource for fine-tuning your approach when you're tirelessly plowing through test after test. Written from the perspective of a test-taker, this book should help guide your entire thought process for each question, start to finish.

- Yoni Stratievsky, Harvard Ready, www.harvardready.com

This LSAT guide is the best tool I could have when preparing for the LSAT. Not only does Graeme do a great job of explaining the sections as a whole, he also offers brilliant explanations for each question. He takes the time to explain why an answer is wrong, which is far more helpful when trying to form a studying pattern.

- Amelia F.

LSAT 72 Explanations
Table Of Contents

Introduction

The LSAT is a hard test.

The only people who take the LSAT are smart people who did well in University. The LSAT takes the very best students, and forces them to compete.

If the test's difficulty shocked you, this is why. The LSAT is a test designed to be hard for smart people.

That's the bad news. But there's hope. The LSAT is a *standardized* test. It has patterns. It can be learned.

To get better, you have to review your mistakes. Many students write tests and move on, without fully understanding their mistakes.

This is understandable. The LSAC doesn't publish official explanations for most tests. It's hard to be sure why you were wrong.

That's where this book comes in. It's a companion for LSAT 72, the June 2014 LSAT.

This book lets you see where you went wrong. It has a full walk through of each question and of every answer choice. You can use this book to fix your mistakes, and make sure you understand *everything*.

By getting this book, you've shown that you're serious about beating this test. I sincerely hope it helps you get the score you want.

There are a few things that I'd like to highlight.

Logical Reasoning: It can be hard to identify conclusions in LR. You don't get feedback on whether you identified the conclusion correctly.

This book gives you that feedback. I've identified the conclusion and the reasoning for each argument. Try to find these on your own beforehand, and make sure they match mine.

Logic Games: Do the game on your own before looking at my explanation. You can't think about a game unless you're familiar with the rules. Once you read my explanations, draw my diagrams yourself on a sheet of paper. You'll understand them much better by recopying them.

Reading Comprehension: You should form a mental map of the passage. This helps you locate details quickly. Make a 1-2 line summary of each paragraph (it can be a mental summary).

I've written my own summaries for each passage. They show the minimum amount of information that you should know after reading a passage, without looking back.

I've included line references in my explanations. You do not need to check these each time. They're only there in case you aren't sure where something is.

Do these three things, and you can answer most Reading Comprehension questions with ease.:

1. Know the point of the passage.
2. Understand the passage, in broad terms. Reread anything you don't understand.
3. Know where to find details. That's the point of the paragraph summaries. I usually do mine in my head, and they're shorter than what I've written.

Review This Book

Before we start, I'd like to ask you a favor. I'm an independent LSAT instructor. I don't have a marketing budget.

But I do my best to make good guides to the LSAT. If you agree, I would love it if you took two minutes to write a review on amazon.com

People judge a book by its reviews. So if you like this guide you can help others discover it. I'd be very grateful.

Good luck!

Graeme

p.s. I'm a real person, and I want to know how the LSAT goes and what you think of this book. Send me an email at graeme@lsathacks.com!

p.p.s. For more books, check out the further reading section at the back. I'm also offering a free half hour LSAT lesson if you fill out a survey.

How To Use This Book

The word "Hacks" in the title is meant in the sense used by the tech world and Lifehacker: "solving a problem" or "finding a better way".

The LSAT can be beaten, but you need a good method. My goal is for you to use this book to understand your mistakes and master the LSAT.

This book is *not* a replacement for practicing LSAT questions on your own.

You have to try the questions by yourself first. When you review, try to see why you were wrong *before* you look at my explanations.

Active review will teach you to fix your own mistakes. The explanations are there for when you have difficulty solving on a question on your own or when you want another perspective on a question.

When you *do* use the explanations, have the question on hand. These explanations are not meant to be read alone. You should use them to help you think about the questions more deeply.

Most of the logical reasoning explanations are pretty straightforward. Necessary assumption questions are often an exception, so I want to give you some guidance to help you interpret the explanations.

The easiest way to test the right answer on a necessary assumption question is to "negate" it.

You negate a statement by making it false, in the slightest possible way. For example, the negation of "The Yankees will win all their games" is "The Yankees will *not* win all their games (they will lose at least one)."

You *don't* have to say that the Yankees will lose *every* game. That goes too far.

If the negation of an answer choice proves the conclusion wrong, then that answer is *necessary* to the argument, and it's the correct answer.

Often, I negate the answer choices when explaining necessary assumption questions, so just keep in mind why they're negated.

Logic games also deserve special mention.

Diagramming is a special symbolic language that you have to get comfortable with to succeed.

If you just *look* at my diagrams without making them yourself, you may find it hard to follow along. You can only learn a language by using it yourself.

So you will learn *much* more if you draw the diagrams on your own. Once you've seen how I do a setup, try to do it again by yourself.

With constant practice, you *will* get better at diagramming, and soon it will come naturally.

But you must try on your own. Draw the diagrams.

Note that when you draw your own diagrams, you don't have to copy every detail from mine. For example, I often leave off the numbers when I do linear games. I've included them in the book, because they make it easier for you to follow along.

But under timed conditions, I leave out many details so that I can draw diagrams faster. If you practice making drawings with fewer details, they become just as easy to understand.

Keep diagrams as minimal as possible.

If you simply don't *like* the way I draw a certain rule type, then you can substitute in your own style of diagram. Lots of people succeed using different styles of drawing.

Just make sure your replacement is easy to draw consistently, and that the logical effect is the same. I've chosen these diagrams because they are clear, they're easy to draw, and they *keep you from forgetting rules*.

I've included line references to justify Reading Comprehension Answers. Use these only in case you're unsure about an explanation. You don't have to go back to the passage for every line reference.

Short Guide to Logical Reasoning

LR Question Types

Must be True: The correct answer is true.

Most Strongly Supported: The correct answer is probably true.

Strengthen/Weaken: The answer is correct if it even slightly strengthens/weakens the argument.

Parallel Reasoning: The correct answer will mirror the argument's structure exactly. It is often useful to diagram these questions (but not always).

Sufficient Assumption: The correct answer will prove the conclusion. It's often useful to diagram sufficient assumption questions. For example:

The conclusion is: A → D

There is a gap between premises and conclusion:

A   B → C → D   **missing link:** A → B or B̶ → A̶

A → B → C   D   **missing link:** C → D or D̶ → C̶

A → B   C → D   **missing link:** B → C or C̶ → B̶

The right answer will provide the missing link.

Necessary Assumption: The correct answer will be essential to the argument's conclusion. Use the negation technique: If the correct answer is false (negated), then the argument falls apart.
The negation of hot is "not hot" rather than cold.

Here's how to do negations: You just make the idea false. This is not so much about grammar as it is about thinking what the idea is, and a counterexample. E.g.

"All Americans are nice" → "One guy in Arkansas named Bob is sort of mean. Every single other American is always really nice"

The "grammatical" negation is "not all Americans are nice", but it's so much clearer and easier to think in terms of making the idea not true.

Point at Issue: Point at Issue questions require two things. **1.** The two speakers must express an opinion on something. **2.** They must disagree about it.

Flawed Reasoning: The correct answer will be a description of a reasoning error made in the argument. It will often be worded very abstractly.

Practice understanding the answers, right and wrong. Flawed Reasoning answers are very abstract, but they all mean something. Think of examples to make them concrete and easier to understand.

Basic Logic

Take the phrase: "All cats have tails."

"Cats" is the sufficient condition. Knowing that something is a cat is "sufficient" for us to say that it has a tail. "Tails" is a necessary condition, because you can't be a cat without a tail. You can draw this sentence as C → T

The **contrapositive** is a correct logical deduction, and reads "anything without a tail is not a cat." You can draw this as T̶ → C̶. Notice that the terms are reversed, and negated.

Incorrect Reversal: "Anything with a tail is a cat." This is a common logical error on the LSAT.

T → C   (Wrong! Dogs have tails and aren't cats.)

Incorrect Negation: "If it is not a cat, it doesn't have a tail." This is another common error.

C̶ → T̶ (Wrong! Dogs aren't cats, but have tails.)

General Advice: Always remember what you are looking for on each question. The correct answer on a strengthen question would be incorrect on a weaken question.

Watch out for subtle shifts in emphasis between the stimulus and the incorrect answer choices. An example would be the difference between "how things are" and "how things should be."

Justify your answers. If you're tempted to choose an answer choice that says something like the sentence below, then be sure you can fill in the blank:

Answer Choice Says: "The politician attacked his opponents' characters",

Fill In The Blank: "The politician said _____ about his opponents' characters."

If you cannot say what the attack was, you can't pick that answer. This applies to many things. You must be able to show that the stimulus supports your idea.

A Few Logic Games Tips

Rule 1: When following along with my explanations....draw the diagrams yourself, too!

This book will be much more useful if you try the games by yourself first. You must think through games on your own, and no book will do that for you. You must have your mind in a game to solve it.

Use the explanations when you find a game you can't understand on your own, or when you want to know how to solve a game more efficiently.

Some of the solutions may seem impossible to get on your own. It's a matter of practice. When you learn how to solve one game efficiently, solving other games becomes easier too.

Try to do the following when you solve games:

Work With What Is Definite: Focus on what must be true. Don't figure out every possibility.

Draw Your Deductions: Unsuccessful students often make the same deductions as successful students. But the unsuccessful students forget their deductions, 15 seconds later! I watch this happen.

Draw your deductions, or you'll forget them. Don't be arrogant and think this doesn't happen to you. It would happen to *me* if I didn't draw my deductions.

Draw Clear Diagrams: Many students waste time looking back and forth between confusing pictures. They've done everything right, but can't figure out their own drawings!

You should be able to figure out your drawings 3 weeks later. If you can't, then they aren't clear enough. I'm serious: look back at your old drawings. Can you understand them? If not, you need a more consistent, cleaner system.

Draw Local Rules: When a question gives you a new rule (a local rule), draw it. Then look for deductions by combining the new rule with your existing rules. Then double-check what you're being asked and see if your deduction is the right answer. This works 90% of the time for local rule questions. And it's fast.

If you don't think you have time to draw diagrams for each question, practice drawing them faster. It's a learnable skill, and it pays off.

Try To Eliminate a Few Easy Answer Choices First: You'll see examples in the explanations that show how certain deductions will quickly get rid of 1-3 answer choices on many questions. This saves time for harder answer choices and it frees up mental space.

You don't have to try the answer choices in order, without thinking about them first.

Split Games Into Two Scenarios When Appropriate: If a rule only allows something to be one of two ways (e.g. F is in 1 or 7), then draw two diagrams: one with F in 1, and one with F in 7. This leads to extra deductions surprisingly often. And it always makes the game easier to visualize.

Combine Rules To Make Deductions: Look for variables that appear in multiple rules. These can often be combined. Sometimes there are no deductions, but it's a crime not to look for them.

Reread The Rules: Once you've made your diagram, reread the rules. This lets you catch any mistakes, which are fatal. It doesn't take very long, and it helps you get more familiar with the rules.

Draw Rules Directly On The Diagram: Mental space is limited. Three rules are much harder to remember than two. When possible, draw rules on the diagram so you don't have to remember them.

Memorize Your Rules: You should memorize every rule you can't draw on the diagram. It doesn't take long, you'll go faster, and you'll make fewer mistakes. Try it, it's not that hard.

If you spend 30 seconds doing this, you'll often save a minute by going through the game faster.

You should also make a numbered list of rules that aren't on the diagram, in case you need to check them.

Section I – Reading Comprehension
Passage 1 – Forest Fires
Questions 1–6

Paragraph Summaries

1. Too much firefighting can be bad. Forests, such as ancient ponderosa forests, have regular cycles of fire. Most large trees survived these fires, and the fires cleared away brush.
2. If there are no fires, fuel builds up. Then when there is a fire, the whole forest can be destroyed.
3. Three factors cause fires: Topography, weather and fuel. Only fuel can be controlled by firefighters. They can reduce fuel by selective harvesting and controlled fires. Once fuel is reduced, there should be maintenance fires every 15-20 years.

Analysis

This passage has a lot of details. It's important for you to have two things:

1. A good understanding and summary of the argument.
2. A grasp of the details. You don't need to memorize them, but you should know roughly where they are.

The argument can be summarized like this:

"If we stop all wildfires, fuels burn up in forests. This eventually leads to devastating fires. We should reduce excess fuel, and then allow controlled burns to periodically clear fuel from forests."

If you understand that, then you can get most questions.

Next, a word about details. I said you shouldn't intentionally memorize details. But that doesn't mean you can forget everything.

When I do a passage, I remember a lot of details without trying, just because I read carefully, and reread if I don't understand. I also skim the passage before starting. This all helps retention.

Knowing many details helps you sift through answers faster. You can judge what matches the passage, and what is put there as a trap.

Now, let's talk about the subject of the passage. This passage is based on real life, by the way. In North America, we've prevented forest fires from happening. So our forests have lots of small trees and deadwood.

When a fire does happen and we can't stop it, the fire quickly grows out of control. It burns everything, even the large trees. The forest can die entirely. This isn't how forests used to work. In the past, fires occurred at regular intervals. The fires killed small trees, and removed deadwood. But the large trees survived.

Deadwood and small trees are what allow fires to grow. If you've ever made a campfire, you'll know that the big logs won't burn right away. You need to light smaller branches that let the fire burn strongly before the big logs will catch fire. Likewise, the large trees in forests only burn because smaller trees and deadwood let the fire burn strong enough.

So if we stop small fires, then fuel builds up in forests and when fires do happen, they are intense. The passage says that many North American forests now have an excess of fuel. So we currently can't let fires happen. They'd be too strong. Instead, we have to clear small trees and deadwood from forests. Once enough fuel is cleared, fires will be less intense.

So *after* we've cleared enough fuel, we can start controlled burns, and let natural fires burn if conditions are damp enough. These periodic fires will clear brush, meaning we will no longer have the problem of excess fuel buildup in forests.

Question 1

DISCUSSION: The purpose of the passage is to describe a problem in forest management (paragraphs 1 and 2) and recommend a solution (paragraph 3).

———————————

A. The passage never talked about ideology. And the author never said anyone is resisting the change. It's possible that everyone wants to fix the forest fire problem. Our current situation could have simply been the result of a mistake, rather than any partisan ideology.

B. The passage doesn't describe two different policies that have been put into place. The passage describes the results of *one* policy that has been in place (stopping all fires). Then the passage recommends putting another policy into place (fuel reduction and controlled burns). Only the first policy has actually been in place.

C. The passage never mentions funding.

D. **CORRECT.** Paragraphs 1 and 2 show that current policy has had bad results – forests are powder kegs that may suffer massive fires. The policy change is in paragraph 3: remove excess fuel and then allow periodic forest fires.

E. This answer describes a completely different situation. There's no contradiction in the recommended policy. Allowing controlled forest fires isn't contradictory to the goal of avoiding destructive fires. Instead, it *supports* the goal of avoiding destructive fires.

Also, if this were the right answer, then the passage would have started by describing the new policy and the apparent contradiction. Instead, the passage started by describing the problems of the old policy.

Question 2

DISCUSSION: Reread around line 55 for the full context of this question. The author is recommending two steps:

1. Reduce excess fuel, so that fires won't be horribly destructive.
2. Once excess fuel is removed, allow maintenance burns every 15-20 years.

It sounds like the periodic fires every 15-20 years will *maintain* the lower level of fuel in the forests.

Lines 50-54 describe these fires. They're either controlled burns we set ourselves, or fires caused by lightning when conditions are damp.

———————————

A. Not quite, though I can see how this is tempting. "Maintenance burns" doesn't just refer to the old style of fire. If it did, then we would never set fires, and we would allow lightning fires to burn even if conditions were dry. Lines 50-54 show that the author instead recommends intentional fires, and letting lightning fires burn only when conditions are damp.

B. The author recommends reducing the density of young, small trees. Mature trees are the ones we want to leave standing. See lines 12-14.

C. Modern North American forests have too much fuel. If we allow fires to occur before we remove fuel, they fires will be very destructive. See lines 27-31.

D. No fires used to occur at intervals "greater than 50 years". 50 years is only referenced in line 30 – it's the length of time we have *prevented* fires from occurring in forests.

E. **CORRECT.** See lines 50-54. They say that maintenance burns are fires that we set and control, or lightning fires that we allow to burn when conditions are damp.

Question 3

DISCUSSION: The first two paragraphs describe how modern forest management has made forests vulnerable to devastating crown fires.

The third paragraphs describes a two step solution:

1. In the short term, remove excess fuel by brush clearing.
2. In the long term, allowed controlled fires to keep fuel at low levels.

To continue the paragraph, the answer should be related to this two part solution or it's likely results.

All the wrong answers introduce new topics. The third paragraph is unlikely to introduce a new topic at the very end of the passage.

A. The passage never talked about damage to homes. The third paragraph is unlikely to introduce a new topic right at the end.
B. The passage never said that any foresters resist these proposals. The third paragraph is unlikely to introduce a new topic right at the end.
C. **CORRECT.** This is a valid continuation. Paragraphs 1 and 2 described the dangers of our present situation. Paragraph 3 described a solution. This answer cautions that the danger described in paragraphs 1 and 2 will still be with us for at least several years, even if we implement the solution.
D. The passage never mentioned economic impacts and it did not mention timber companies. The third paragraph is unlikely to introduce new topics right at the end.
E. The passage never talked about financial resources or whether this proposal could be implemented in practice. The third paragraph is unlikely to introduce a new topic right at the end.

Question 4

DISCUSSION: Look at lines 36-41. They say that there are three relevant factors: topography, weather and fuel.

We can only control fuel, so that's where we should focus.

A. **CORRECT.** Read lines 39-41 in particular. They say that fuel is the only one of the three elements we can control, so we should focus there.
B. This contradicts the passage. The point of the third paragraph is to show that we *can* control wildfires and help forests return to a healthier state with less fuel.
C. Nonsense. It's paragraphs 1 and 2 that show why forests fires are more destructive.
D. This is total nonsense. It takes words used in the passage, and combines them in a way that doesn't have much meaning. Lines 36-40 were fairly clear, and they have nothing to do with this answer.
There's nothing much else to say except to point out that the passage did not argue that specific fuel types are dependent on weather.
E. Lightning is part of weather. But that's as far as this goes. Read lines 39-41. They explain the purpose of the three factors: we can only control fuel, so we should focus there.

Question 5

DISCUSSION: Ancient ponderosa forests are described in the first paragraph. Here's what we know about them:

- They had low intensity fires.
- They were open forests.
- They had low levels of fuel.
- Mature trees survived fires.
- Fires cleared the forests of young trees.

These facts are all in lines 11-14; I've just summarized them. The right answer will likely be one of these facts.

Lines 15-20 also say that ponderosa forests had small fires at intervals between 5-20 years.

———————————

A. The passage never mentions modern ponderosas or genetics. You're not looking for something that might be true in real life, you're looking for something the passage actually said.
B. CORRECT. This is fairly well supported. Line 14 says the fires cleared the forests of young trees. Fewer trees = lower population density. Modern ponderosa forests don't have fires, as we have stopped wildfires over the past 50 years (line 30). Therefore, since modern forests have more young trees, the population density is likely higher.
C. The passage never mentions weather patterns in ponderosa forests or if weather has changed over time.
D. We know that fires reduce the *number* of trees. We don't know if fires reduce the *diversity* of trees. Unless a fire makes a tree species disappear from the forest entirely, the forest diversity stays the same.
E. The passage only said large fires kill wildlife (line 24). The passage never mentions whether low intensity fires affect or control wildlife.

Question 6

DISCUSSION: Lines 51-54 mention lightning fires. We should allow them to burn, but only if forests are damp, and only once fuel has been cleared from forests. (See lines 45-49 – we must clear fuel before we can have low intensity fires again).

So the author would think it is a mistake to allow all lightning fires to burn.

———————————

A. No. See the discussion above. It is not wise to allow all lightning fires to burn.
B. Same as A. It is not a good idea to allow *all* lightning fires to burn. See the discussion above.
C. This is not supported. In North America, many forests currently have an excess of fuel. If fires burn, those forests will be destroyed. We must clear fuel before allowing fires. This is lines 45-49: clearing brush recreates the conditions that allow for low-intensity burns.
So *no* forests benefit from lightning fires until excess fuel has been cleared. Further, the passage didn't really make a distinction between old and young forests. The passage only talks about old and young *trees,* within the same forest.
D. CORRECT. Lines 51-54 support this. We should only allow lightning fires when "weather is damp enough to reduce the risk of extensive damage".
E. The passage never talks about public perception or whether the recommended policy is politically feasible.

Passage 2 – Mali and UNESCO
Questions 7–13

Paragraph Summaries

1. Mali prevented the sale of sculptures from Djenne-jeno, but it couldn't finance any legal excavations or protect the site. So the sites were looted.
2. UNESCO regulations support the idea that cultures own artifacts from their history. (So Mali was right to want to control their artifacts)
3. Unfortunately, regulations encourage excavators to avoid documenting the artifacts they take.
4. It would have been better if Mali had licensed excavations as long as the artifacts were documented and the excavators paid tax.

Analysis

This passage is an argument. First, it describes a bad situation: artifacts have been looted from Mali. Next, it describes UNESCO regulations that condemn such looting and show that Mali is the rightful owner of the artifacts.

Then the argument takes a twist. It seems the regulations themselves helped ensure the looting erases history, because it gave owners an incentive to hide evidence of looting. The argument recommends regulating and allowing more excavations, in exchange for taxes and information.

I think the argument is actually pretty clear, but that may be my background knowledge in economics. If you found this passage difficult, the Economist magazine has much reading material in this style. (Take their opinions with a grain of salt, but they'll help get you used to this subject matter).

Put yourself in the shoes of a smuggler. Under the current system, you're going to hide all evidence that you stole artifacts from Mali. You're not going to write down any information about the artifacts you dig up. Apart from you and the buyer, no one will know the artifacts exist.

This is bad. Lines 30-34 show that one of the reasons for the UNESCO rules is that we want to learn about the history of artifacts. Ideally, when you excavate an artifact, you should give details about where you found the object, describe other objects nearby, and record your find in some registry with photos and a description.

Right now, there is no incentive for smugglers to record any information. We can say "this is bad, it should stop!". But while it feels good to condemn smuggling, it won't stop smuggling. There's a large demand for artifacts, so unless you stop *that*, smugglers will steal artifacts.

The fourth paragraph proposes a solution: allow the legal sale of artifacts. But in exchange, the excavators must record information and pay a tax.

At face value, this does seem like a better solution. Almost anything would be! Right now, everything has been looted and we don't know where it is. The knowledge of this ancient civilization is permanently lost.

Of course, lines 51-54 do point out that professional excavators could record even more information. If Mali had the resources to fund excavation and enforce the law, this would be a better solution. But Mali *doesn't* have those resources, which is why the author proposes their solution.

Note that the passage is making an argument about what countries like Mali should do to preserve their artifacts. It's too late for Mali, the artifacts are gone. However, for simplicity, in the questions I'm going to refer to what "Mali" should do, as it's far shorter to write and read.

Question 7

DISCUSSION: The passage discusses how we can achieve the goals of the UNESCO regulations (preserving information about artifacts and ensuring cultural ownership of artifacts) despite limited resources and looting.

The author recommends allowing some excavations in exchange for information and taxes.

A. This answer sort of sounds like paragraph 2, but it doesn't describe it accurately.
This answer totally misses the main point of the passage: looting, and how to manage it.

B. CORRECT. This describes everything.
Paragraph 1 is the failure of preservation.
Paragraphs 1, 2 and 3 describe the laws prohibiting export, and the consequences.
Paragraph 4 describes the more flexible solution: allow legal excavations.

C. Nonsense. This answer plays on American fears of international institutions. Those are outside assumptions that have nothing to do with the passage. Mali passed laws voluntarily, and agrees with UNESCO's position.

D. This contradicts the passage. The fourth paragraph suggests licensing more than accredited archaeologists. See lines 51-54, they imply professionals won't be the only excavators.

E. Tempting, but this isn't quite right. The author doesn't think Mali should give up ownership of the artifacts. The author thinks Mali should change how it allows others to use the artifacts. Currently, there is a total ban on excavation, but the author thinks there should be some legal excavations. (paragraph 4.)

This might have been right if it said: "The total prohibition on legal excavation, inspired by international regulations, does more harm than good in countries like Mali."

Question 8

DISCUSSION: See lines 22-25. They're the only lines that say how countries have used UNESCO regulations. Some countries have said all antiquities belong to the state and cannot be exported.

All the wrong answers describe things the passage never mentions. They might be true in real life, or good ideas, but that's not what you're looking for.

A. The author might think this is a good idea, but that's not what you're looking for. You're looking for something that the passage said countries have actually done, and the passage doesn't say any countries have done this.

B. CORRECT. Lines 22-25 say this directly.

C. Same as A. The author might think this is a good idea, but that's not what you're looking for. You're looking for something that countries have done, and the passage doesn't say any countries have done this.

D. The passage never says any countries have done this. It's *true*, in the real world, that some cultures spill across national boundaries. But you're looking for ways that countries have used the UNESCO doctrine, according to the passage.

E. Unfortunately, the passage never says that any countries have tried to preserve artifacts in countries like Mali.

Question 9

DISCUSSION: You'll want to reread the whole fourth paragraph to answer this question. (It shouldn't take long, rereading is much faster than reading).

This question is basically asking: what was the author's plan in the fourth paragraph. The tax was part of their overall plan.

The purpose of the tax is to fund acquisitions of artifacts. If you just keep reading line 51, you'll see the sentence says this. A *lot* of reading comprehension questions that quote specific lines can be answered if you just go back and read the entire sentence.

The best answer is C. The tax is indeed "one part" of the author's more pragmatic approach.

––––––––––––

A. The author did say the artifacts should be acquired for the museum. But that's all we know – the author didn't say anything about the museum's role in preserving artifacts.
B. The author is proposing a hypothetical, future policy. Unfortunately, Mali's past policies didn't work. Mali's policies led to the looting of the country's artifacts, we say this in paragraph 1.
C. **CORRECT.** The tax + acquisition idea is one part of a larger plan to document and preserve Mali's artifacts by allowing some legal excavations.
D. No, a different part of the passage describes the incentive for documentation. Lines 44-47 say that artifacts have greater value when documented, which is a good reason for owners to want documentation. Taxes have nothing to do with documentation.
E. *Paragraph 3* is the part of the passage that highlights the flaw in UNESCO doctrine: the regulations discourage documentation. The tax is not a flaw in the doctrine.

Question 10

DISCUSSION: The author thinks the UNESCO regulations are well intentioned (see paragraph 2 and lines 30-31 "painful irony"). However, the author believes that the UNESCO regulations have the unfortunate effect of discouraging documentation of artifacts (paragraph 3).

––––––––––––

A. **CORRECT.** The fourth paragraph and lines 41-47 support this. The author is proposing a way that UNESCO *could* help countries like Mali.
B. Nonsense. This gets things backwards. UNESCO made regulations, and countries like Mali made laws that were in accord with the regulations. See lines 21-25 – many countries used the regulations to justify laws.
C. The passage never talks about laws or initiatives that cover multiple states.
D. The author never says that Mali has concerns that UNESCO ignored. In fact, the passage suggests that UNESCO completely supports Mali. The problem is that countries like Mali lack resources to enforce laws or fund excavations.
E. We know *Mali* had inadequate funding. But the passage never says UNESCO has inadequate funding. Maybe UNESCO has lots of money. But UNESCO doesn't have jurisdiction to enforce Mali's laws, so UNESCO's money might be of no use in preventing looting.

Question 11

DISCUSSION: The right answer on this type of question is almost always directly supported by a line from the passage.

A. The author doesn't say this. In fact, lines 51-54 imply that non-archaeologists would be allowed to do excavations.

B. The fourth paragraph contradicts this. There, the author suggests allowing the export of artifacts. The key concern seems to be preserving history and documenting artifacts.

C. CORRECT. See lines 54-56. Those lines say that not everyone would obey the law, but that the new proposal is still better than what's happening now.

D. The author never describes punishments. Unfortunately, right now Mali is unable to enforce the law (lines 3-4) so it's unclear is punishments are possible.

E. This is playing on a common American idea about regulations: they should be simple. You're not looking thing that might be true in the real world – you're looking for things in the passage. The passage says *nothing* about simple regulations. It's fine to use outside knowledge to judge some answers, but you can't use it to make stuff up.

Question 12

DISCUSSION: As with question 11, the right answer on this type of question is almost always directly supported by a line from the passage.

The wrong answers either contradict the passage, or never appear in the passage.

A. This contradicts the passage. The author says some artifacts should be bought for the museum (lines 49-51), but she actually recommends allowing the export of many artifacts, in the fourth paragraph.

B. Same as A. Line 49 says objects can be exported.

C. The passage never says this. It's true the author recommends allowing private ownership. But that's just part of a pragmatic plan to preserve history. The author never says that artifacts are "too valuable" to be owned by the state.

D. CORRECT. Lines 51-54 suggest that experts should excavate when possible. Professional archaeologists preserve the most information, and the author thinks preserving information is important.

E. The author doesn't say this. The fourth paragraph says Mali has trusteeship (a form of ownership) of the artifacts, and should *license* them to others (lines 41-45). Mali owns the artifacts, but *allows* others to excavate and use them.

Question 13

DISCUSSION: I got his question wrong when I did this test timed. I chose E. It was a big stretch. I knew the author understood why the collectors wanted terra-cotta. I twisted this into meaning that she had sympathy ("understand of") their motives.

This was wrong. The lesson is that reading comprehension answers are almost never a stretch. Instead, you can typically find a line that proves the answer. I had trouble on this question because I totally missed the line that answers the question, even when I looked back.

This question is absurdly easy if you noticed the line. On line 8, the author says collectors "rightly admire" the terra-cotta sculptures. That means she thinks the collectors have good taste in sculpture.

Any opinion words such as "rightly" are extremely important to take note of. I failed in this case.

A. You might have picked this because paragraph 4 talks about how excavators can help preserve artifacts. But paragraph 4 was *hypothetical*. So far, excavators have done nothing but harm. See paragraph 1.

B. CORRECT. Line 8 says collectors "rightly admire" the sculptures. This shows the author approves of the aesthetic (i.e. artistic) judgement of the collectors.

C. Ridiculous. The collectors are the ones buying illegally exported artifacts. Why would the author expect them to take action against themselves? Maybe you thought this answer said dismay at Mali or UNESCO's failure to take action?

D. The author never said this. In fact, the author doesn't talk about the people of Mali at all. I doubt the people of Mali are particularly concerned about the artifacts. Most people in most countries don't care too much about artifacts. They have other priorities.

E. The author understands why collectors want terra-cotta sculptures, and she understands why they don't document their finds. That *doesn't* mean she approves of (has sympathy with) their motives.

Passage 3 – Equipoise
Questions 14–21

Paragraph Summaries

1. There is a contradiction between the ethical requirement to provide the best treatment, and the research requirement to have no opinion about the best treatment. (Equipoise)
2. "Theoretical" equipoise is too strict. It requires clinicians to have *no* preference for one of two treatments. This is almost impossible.
3. "Clinical" equipoise is more realistic. Clinicians can ethically participate in a study if the research community is split on what drug may be more effective.
4. Divided opinion about the effects of drugs is what makes clinical equipoise ethically possible.

Analysis

This is the hardest passage on the test. Equipoise is not a word you hear most days. I took this opportunity to look it up:

Equipoise: balance of forces or interests

In other words, ethics requires researchers to believe that both treatments have an equal chance of succeeding.

Before I explain the passage, I want to talk a bit about science. The LSAT expects you to have two kinds of scientific knowledge:

1. An understanding of how experiments work.
2. A basic background knowledge of scientific material that prevents your head from spinning when you read science passages and LR science questions.

Technically, the second kind of knowledge isn't essential. You don't need subject matter knowledge to get LSAT questions right. But oh how it helps! The LSAT is based on real world situations, and subject knowledge is incredibly useful.

I actually find science passages are *easier* than average (even this one wasn't bad) because I have a good baseline amount of scientific knowledge.

To improve both types of scientific knowledge, I recommend reading the science section of the Economist. It talks about scientific topics in a way that's not dumbed down, and yet makes sense for a non-scientist.

Go to your local library, and get 20-30 back issues of the Economist. I say 20-30 because the science section is small – each issue only has 2-3 pages.

Also, get the print magazine. Don't read it online. For two reasons. First, the LSAT is in print, so it's better to match the format. Second, the Economist website has many blog posts. These don't have the same style as the science articles in the print magazine, which are better for our purposes.

Once you read a sufficient amount of scientific material, you will have a better scientific background and you'll be able to understand what's going on in science passages. You'll also gain an intuition for how experiments are supposed to work.

Now, to the passage itself. I'm going explain it with an example. I'll talk about HIV and anti-retrovirals. HIV is, of course, the horrible, currently incurable disease that leads to AIDS.

We don't know how to cure HIV. But we currently can manage it with anti-retrovirals. As far as we know, these are the best treatment option for HIV.

But surely there may be a better option. For instance, maybe a new type of drug will prevent HIV turning into AIDS, with fewer side effects than anti-retrovirals (I'm assuming they have some side effects, most drugs do). Or maybe another drug will cure HIV entirely.

So, we want to be able to test new drugs to see if they are better than anti-retrovirals. But, the problem here is that there is a conflict between these two ethical standards:

1. Doctors should prescribe the best treatment.
2. Professionals conducting experiments should be neutral about the likely results of the experiment.

Currently, professionals believe that anti-retrovirals are the best treatment. So they're ethically obligated to prescribe then. But this makes it very hard to be neutral about which treatment will be best – the ' medical community will tend to favor anti-retrovirals. It's hard to be neutral about a new treatment when that treatment doesn't have the same number of studies that anti-retrovirals do.

Now, theoretical equipoise does have some uses. It rightly prevents doctors from testing good solutions against alternatives that everyone expects will be useless. For instance, it is rightly ethically impossible to conduct an experiment that compares anti-retrovirals and salt as cures for HIV. No one believes salt cures HIV (I think). So it would be grossly unethical to deny half of the experiment access to life saving drugs in order to measure the difference between anti-retrovirals and salt.

That's clear. But what if there was a trial between anti-retrovirals and a promising but unproven drug? Most doctors would think that anti-retrovirals are a better treatment, until they see evidence. But they can only get evidence by doing a study.

Under current ethical standards, it's very hard to do a new study. If the doctors think the new drug is unlikely to be better, it's unethical to prescribe it to half of the experiment, even if it's less unethical than prescribing something obviously useless (such as salt).

If doctors are required to be strictly neutral when conducting an experiment (theoretical equipoise) then it's almost impossible to test new drugs. the new drugs might be better, but at the time the experiment starts no reasonable doctor would believe that.

That's why the author proposes a new standard: clinical equipoise. This allows researchers to ethically test two drugs if at least some part of the medical community believes each drug is effective.

So we might have a case where 95% of a community thinks anti-retrovirals are best, but 5% of the community thinks that the new drug is better. In that case, researchers could ethically test both drugs, since there is some support for favoring the new drug.

Note that this only works for new drugs that have some support. If a new drug has some promise, but *no* part of the medical community thinks it is best, then even clinical equipoise won't let researchers ethically prescribe the new drug.

Note that "community" refers to a specific group of doctors and researchers who are experts about a given type of drug or disease. One of the questions asks about this.

Question 14

DISCUSSION: The point of the passage is to argue for less strict ethical standards for how to conduct clinical trials. We should allow researchers to have an opinion about which treatment is best, as long as they recognize that others disagree.

_____

A. This passage is not an explanation. It's an *argument*. The author is arguing we should use clinical equipoise instead of theoretical equipoise.

B. **CORRECT.** See lines 33-36. This is the conclusion of the argument: we should develop a new, more relaxed standard called clinical equipoise.

C. Nonsense. The author is the one proposing a change! They hope the change will help us do more trials.
Also, the passage never mentions that equipoise affects our ability to derive information from trials. Instead, equipoise affects whether we can do a trial in the first place.

D. I don't even know what this answer means. How could it possibly be the main point? What is a "conception embodied in an ethical standard"? That could mean many things.

E. Careful. It is true that the passage "argues for a change". But the rest of the answer is wrong. Equipoise refers to the attitude researchers have about the effectiveness of different methods. It doesn't affect how researchers "gather data" in a trial.

Question 15

DISCUSSION: The second paragraph starts with "unfortunately". This paragraph is describing a problem with theoretical equipoise: it's too strict. Enforcing theoretical equipoise makes it very hard to do studies.

Most wrong answers contradict the passage.

_____

A. Clinical equipoise doesn't even appear until the third paragraph. The second paragraph can't be about clinical equipoise.
Also, there is no conflict between the view in paragraphs two and three. It's all the same view: the author's opinion! It can be summed up as: theoretical equipoise has problems, we should use clinical equipoise.

B. The second paragraph actually never says what factors lead doctors to prefer one treatment over another.

C. Careful. It's true the second paragraph is attacking theoretical equipoise. But not by "undermining the moral principle" underlying theoretical equipoise. The underlying principle is neutrality, and the author doesn't think there's anything wrong with that, in principle.
The second paragraph instead undermines theoretical equipoise *in practice*.

D. **CORRECT.** The main difficulty is a practical one. The second paragraph explains why theoretical equipoise is almost impossible to apply in the real world.

E. The author doesn't think there is an *inherent* conflict of interest in equipoise. If researchers truly believed two treatments were equally likely to be the best, then there would be no problem testing them.
There's only a conflict when physicians believe one treatment is better *but* are also required to believe both treatments are equal.

Question 16

DISCUSSION: The right answer will actually be in the passage. You should try to find a line reference.

Most of the wrong answers sound tempting because they use words from the passage, but in reality they actually contradict the passage.

———————————

A. Not quite. Theoretical equipoise may only be *one* ethical requirement for doing a study. There could be many other factors that can make a study unethical.

B. This is true in the real world, but the passage never mentions it. You're not looking for something you may recognize from outside knowledge. You're looking for something the passage says.

C. **CORRECT.** Lines 50-56 say this directly. You can participate ethically in a study while believing one of the two treatments is better.

D. The whole point of the passage is that theoretical equipoise is much more strict than clinical equipoise! If you picked this, you either misunderstood the answer or you need to reread the passage.

E. This is unlikely. The author has just *invented* the idea of clinical equipoise. It doesn't exist yet! See lines 34-36. ("A new notion should be developed....")

Question 17

DISCUSSION: The difference between theoretical and clinical equipoise is this: theoretical equipoise requires strict neutrality. Clinical equipoise allows you to have an opinion as long as a substantial part of the community thinks otherwise.

How to violate theoretical equipoise: Not being neutral.

How to violate clinical equipoise: Not being neutral AND not believing that some of the medical community disagrees.

I should clarify about clinical equipoise. It doesn't work if there is no disagreement. The reason you can have a bias under clinical equipoise is that you recognize that some part of the community disagrees with you. So if no part of the community thinks the other drug is better, clinical equipoise is impossible.

Neutrality is permissible under both standards. Neutrality does not violate clinical equipoise!

———————————

A. This might violate both types of equipoise. Clinical equipoise requires disagreement. Here the results are so striking that it sounds like few researchers favor the second treatment. ("Most" can include "all" or "almost all".)

B. This trial sounds like it meets the standards of both theoretical and clinical equipoise. If both treatments seem equal, then it's possible for researchers to be neutral.

C. This violates theoretical equipoise. Researchers are required to be neutral. This also may violate clinical equipoise. If scientists aren't neutral, then clinical equipoise requires part of the community to disagree about what treatment is best. See lines 48-50.

D. **CORRECT.** This definitely violates theoretical equipoise. That requires strict neutrality. However, this likely does not violate clinical equipoise. Clinical equipoise allows researchers to have an opinion, as long as they recognize that part of the community disagrees with them. See the final paragraph, especially lines 48-50 and 53-56.

E. If physicians in the trial think the treatments are equal, then these physicians are neutral. So they meet the standards of both types of equipoise.

23

Question 18

DISCUSSION: The "main point" is very similar to the "primary purpose". Actually, I couldn't tell you how the two question types are different. Technically, it's the difference between "what" and "why", so this question is asking "what does the passage say?".

In practice though, just pick the answer that best describes the passage and its argument. The author's point is that we should use a less strict standard: clinical equipoise.

The passage is an *argument*. Some of the answers are merely descriptive. The right answer should say that the passage makes a recommendation.

Also, remember that an answer is not right just because it's true. A couple answers are true, but they do not describe the main point.

A. Not quite. Strict equipoise doesn't jeopardize any ethical standards. Instead, it jeopardizes our ability to conduct experiments.

B. I was tempted by this. But the argument is not talking about ethical requirements in general. Instead, it's talking about clinical vs. theoretical equipoise.
Further, the passage is not descriptive. The passage is an *argument*. But this answer is merely descriptive.

C. This is *true*, according to the passage, but you're not looking for what's true. The point of the passage was to argue for a different ethical standard.

D. CORRECT. This correctly describes the passage as an argument. The author's point was that we should use clinical rather than theoretical equipoise, which was unnecessarily restrictive.

E. This is not really a good description of the passage. This might be *true*, according to the passage, but we're looking for the main point. The point is not just that theoretical equipoise is inadequate. Instead, the point is that we should use clinical equipoise.

Question 19

DISCUSSION: The full line says "expert clinical community". From context, this probably refers to a group of doctors and researchers with experience in certain drugs and diseases.

For instance, the community of HIV/AIDS researchers or the community of throat cancer researchers. These researchers may be spread all over the world – research communities aren't usually based on geography.

A. CORRECT. This is it. For instance, the HIV/AIDS research community focusses on how to cure and treat HIV/AIDS. Their body of knowledge is common clinical experience and published research on how to treat HIV/AIDS.

B. Doubtful. Medical experts live all over the world yet work on the same problems. Nothing in the passage suggests a geographic community of researchers.

C. This doesn't have to be true. For instance, I'm sure the HIV/AIDS community has many opinions on topics I have *no* opinion about, because I am unfamiliar with the topic. It's not a requirement that a community differ in opinion from other communities. The community just needs to be studying the same topic.

D. This answer throws in the term "ethics" to try to confuse you. It's true the passage is talking about the ethics of conducting experiments. But that's a specific context. A community doesn't have to have the same ethical opinions on all topics (e.g. should you give to charity? Do we owe a responsibility to family than to strangers?)

E. What an odd answer. The passage doesn't talk about research methods, or methods being used in multiple disciplines. (An ethical requirement in an experiment is not a research method).

Question 20

DISCUSSION: The right answer is directly supported by the passage. This is almost always the case on reading comprehension "must be true" questions. You can save time by finding a line reference rather than getting stuck between answers.

A. We're never told about any actual clinical trials and whether they meet any standards.
B. This is tempting, but it isn't necessarily true. Lines 29-32 say that *if* theoretical equipoise is adhered to, few trials would start. So there are two possibilities:
1. Few trials start.
2. Many trials start, but they violate theoretical equipoise.

This answer only works if we can rule out the second possibility. And we can't do that.
C. CORRECT. Lines 29-32 suggest this. They say very few clinical trials could achieve theoretical equipoise. So that technically means the standard is rarely met.
D. Careful. Lines 8-14 do say that most clinicians and ethicists think we should use theoretical equipoise. But this answer talks about ethical standards *in general*. We have no idea if clinicians and ethicists think all current ethical standards are good.
E. This is doubtful. Current ethical practice requires neutrality in studies. If there is a conflict in a community, neutrality is difficult. So it's hard for current studies to resolve conflicts *and* obey ethical standards.

Question 21

DISCUSSION: The argument in the third and fourth paragraphs is that we can and should use an alternate ethical standard: clinical equipoise.

A. CORRECT. Read lines 48-50. Clinical equipoise depends on disagreement within the expert community. For clinical equipoise to work, at least some people must think the alternative treatment is best.
If there is a consensus that one treatment is better, then it would be unethical to conduct a trial to confirm that fact, even if clinical equipoise was the standard. That's because it's unethical to prescribe a treatment you believe to be worse (lines 1-2), so it would be unethical for researchers to prescribe the treatment that a consensus of experts believed was worse.
B. This supports the idea of equipoise. If few researchers feel conflicted, then equipoise is *easier*. *(Clinical equipoise offers a way to run trial without neutrality, but neutrality is *even better* if possible.)*
C. This doesn't really weaken the argument in paragraphs 3 and 4. It just indicates a problem with medical trials generally.
This is like saying a proposal to reform the police department is wrong because crime is rising. Rising crime is a problem, certainly, but the reorganization might still be good idea. Likewise, adopting clinical equipoise might be a good idea even if there are other problems with medical trials.
D. Who cares what ethicists think? They might be wrong! On the LSAT, we're concerned with what *is* true, not with what people *think* is true.
Normally, you should give some deference to experts, but this passage provides much evidence that ethicists have used standards that aren't helpful.
E. This doesn't really matter. Developing a bias during a trial is only one way to violate theoretical equipoise. Researchers can also have a bias at the start of a trial: the third and fourth paragraph describe this possibility. Having a bias at the start of a trial is the main reason for clinical equipoise, and this answer doesn't weaken that reason.

Passage 4 – Flat Tax (comparative)
Questions 22–27

Paragraph Summaries

Passage A

1. A flat tax with no deductions seems to work in Estonia.
2. Some say flat taxes are unfair. Some believe that flat taxes will tax the rich less than our current progressive systems do.
3. But flat taxes can have thresholds below which no taxes are paid. Also, normal tax systems have deductions. High income earners usually end up paying about as much under a flat tax.

Passage B

1. It's a myth that you pay more on your existing income by moving to a higher tax bracket. Progressive taxes treat people equally. (See analysis for detailed discussion.)
2. The poorer you are, the more useful an extra dollar is.
3. Some flat taxes exempt the poor. That means you jump from no taxes to the highest bracket instantly. Middle class people will pay more from a flat tax.

Analysis

Passage A has muddled logic. There are a few issues we need to disentangle to consider flat taxes. I'm going to start with an overview of taxation. I'll talk about the passages themselves once I clarify the issues.

Flat vs. progressive taxes: In the United States and most of the Western world, taxes are progressive. This is often misunderstood. Let's say you earn $50,000.

Here's how a progressive system might tax your $50,000:

First $10,000: 0%

$20,000 after that: 20%

$20,000 after that: 30%

Anything above $50,000: 40%

People often think that you can *lose* money by increasing your income and moving to the next taxation level. This is false. Whether you earn $50,000 or $1,000,000, your first $50,000 are treated the same. *Everyone* pays no tax on the first $10,000 of income.

So under the system I described, someone with $50,000 pays $10,000 tax. They pay zero on the first $10,000, $4,000 on the next $20,000 (at a 20% rate) and $6,000 on the next $20,000 (at a 30% rate).

So their *average* tax rate is 20%. On their last $20,000 they paid a tax rate of 30%, but they had a lower rate on lower income so that dragged down the average.

The *marginal* tax rate is 40%. That means that any income over $50,000 is taxed at 40%.

So if someone earns $60,000, they pay $10,000 on the first $50,000 (as I calculated above) and then an additional $4,000 on the remaining $10,000, which is the 40% marginal rate.

So their total taxes are $14,000 and their average tax rate is 23.3%. Their marginal rate is still 40%.

Confused yet? This is actually still a simple tax system. I haven't introduced deductions, which come in the next section. But first, let's look at a flat tax.

Let's say a flat tax exempts the first $10,000 of income. You pay no tax on that money. And then you pay 25% on the remaining income, no matter how much you earn.

How much tax does someone earning $50,000 pay? Their first $10,000 is exempt, so they pay 25% tax on the remaining $40,000, which is $10,000.

So under my flat tax system, a $50,000 earner pays exactly the same.

What about someone earning $60,000? They pay the same $10,000 as someone earning $50,000, plus an additional $2,500, which is 25% of their extra $10,000. So they pay $12,500 total. Which is *less* than they paid before.

Who pays more under a flat tax? Someone earning $30,000 or less will pay more under this system. Someone rich will pay much, much less.

Now, you can fiddle the numbers by changing the rates or by increasing the exemption, but generally the poor pay more under a flat tax, average earners pay about the same, and the rich pay less. But the more money you were getting from the rich, the more you'd have to raise taxes on the poor and middle incomes to make up for the lost money from the wealthy.

Passage A skirts this issue of progressive taxation almost entirely. Instead, they focus on deductions.

Deductions: When you pay taxes, you can reduce the amount you pay by claiming deductions. For instance, in America, you can reduce your taxes if you paid interest on a mortgage.

In Canada, I can get a tax deduction if I take public transit and buy a monthly pass. There are deductions for all kinds of things. Governments love deductions because they make governments look good, and because deductions don't cost money directly.

But a large number of deductions make the tax code more complex. America has a vast number of deductions, far more than Canada. This is the reason your tax returns are complicated. Canadian taxes, for a regular employee, are incredibly simple and can be finished in an hour or two.

In passage A, the flat tax removed all deductions. This has the effect of considerably simplifying the tax code. This is, generally, a good thing. Economists of all persuasions tend to agree on this point.

This is also the reason a flat tax might gain more from the rich. Tax deductions tend to be better for the wealthy. They have complex enough financial affairs that they can take advantage of them, and they can also afford an accountant who will find all the deductions that can benefit them.

What Estonia Did

So Estonia's tax reform really did two things. It made the tax system "flat" – there is one rate for everyone. And it also removed all deductions, simplifying the tax code.

These two changes are often proposed together, but they don't have to go together.

Here lies the confusion of passage A. The author argues for a "flat" tax system, but their evidence is based mainly on the benefits of a "simplified" tax system that has no deductions.

Estonia may well have succeeded with their new tax system, but we don't know if it's because it's flat or simplified.

Passage B has a clearer view of what a flat tax system might do. If the rich pay less, it will be the middle that makes up the difference.

Passage A does have a good point about tax evasion. The more taxes you levy on the rich, the more likely they are to try to avoid them (often legally, though certainly not always). So making a simple, flat tax system may actually have the effect *in practice* of raising more money from the rich even if *in theory* a progressive system would get more.

Passage B would be stronger if it addressed this practical issue. Mind you, it's difficult to discuss since we have little real world experience of flat taxes.

Question 22

DISCUSSION: I misread this question and got it wrong as a result. I thought the question stem said "both passages answer which of the following questions?". That's a common reading comprehension question type.

But actually, the question says both passages are "concerned with" answering the question in the right answer. That's a far looser standard – it means both passages aim to discuss the issue in the. Passage B doesn't explicitly say flat taxes are unfair, but the whole passage is most definitely "concerned with" the fairness of taxation systems.

A. Both authors seem to take it for granted that a flat tax can be implemented. So they're not concerned with answering the question.

B. Passage B answers this question in the first paragraph. Passage A does not seem to answer it.

C. CORRECT. Lines 9-17 in passage A are concerned with the fairness of a flat tax system. Passage B is a bit trickier. Paragraph 1 introduces the topic of fairness (related to a progressive tax). Paragraph 2 discusses how dollars are not equal and matter more to the poor. The 3rd paragraph then criticizes flat taxes. Lines 51-53 criticize flat taxes (with a question). Then lines 55-59 say that the rich will pay less and the middle class more. Since the middle class need dollars more than the rich, it's implied that this is unfair.
Passage B is an argument. The first paragraph was about fairness, so it only makes sense to read paragraphs 2 and 3 in terms of fairness.

D. I originally chose this answer. I thought lines 21-25 were passage A's criticism of progressive tax systems (they encourage tax evasion) and I thought lines 30-39 showed passage B responded to some incorrect criticisms of progressive taxation.
The problem is that passage B isn't *concerned with* identifying objections to flat taxes. It's just something they mention by the way. Passage B is concerned with describing how flat taxes are unfair.

E. Passage A says flat taxes reduce avoidance, but passage B never discusses this.

Question 23

DISCUSSION: Remember, the right answer is something that happens in *both* passages. Two of the wrong answers happen in one passage but not both. You should always find line references to justify the right answer, otherwise you risk fooling yourself.

A. Neither author says this. Shifting your ground means you change your argument once someone proves your first argument was wrong.

B. The author of passage A cites the example of Estonia. The author of passage B doesn't cite any real world examples.

C. Neither passage uses analogies. An analogy is when you use one situation to make an argument about a similar situation. Like if I compared athletic training to LSAT prep: you need to track your progress in both sports and the LSAT. That's an analogy between the two subjects.

D. A rhetorical question is one that is not meant to be answered. Passage B uses a rhetorical question in lines 50-54, but passage A doesn't even have a question mark.

E. CORRECT. In passage A, see lines 15-17. The second paragraph is the alleged misunderstanding, and paragraph 3 corrects this: it is possible for flat tax systems to tax the rich as much as progressive systems do.

In passage B, see lines 30-39. The author corrects the misunderstanding that you can lose money by moving to a higher tax bracket.

Question 24

DISCUSSION: Passage B's main argument is that the rich will pay less under a flat tax system, and the middle classes will pay more (see lines 55-58). This contradicts the claim in paragraph 3 of passage A.

Passage A doesn't say outright that the middle classes will not pay more under a flat tax. But paragraphs 2 and 3 of passage A argue that flat taxes can be progressive, and they can raise as much money from the rich as current systems do.

This *implies* but doesn't states that flat taxes should raise as much money from each segment as before. So presumably if the rich are paying as much as before, the middle class should also pay the same amount, if we are raising the same amount of revenue.

The right answer, D, challenges this by showing that the middle class pay more in flat tax countries. This likely means that the rich are paying less (the poor already weren't paying). So this weakens passage A's argument that flat taxes can raise as much from the rich. This answer is a *bit* of a stretch, but it's the best one.

A. Equal revenues don't prove anything. Passage B is talking about *who* pays revenue. Their claim is that the rich will pay less, even if total revenue is the same.
B. This supports passage A. Passage A is arguing for a simple tax code.
C. Who cares what rich people *believe?* The passages are talking about what actually happens. Beliefs are often false.
D. CORRECT. See lines 55-58. This is exactly what the author of passage B predicted. They thought the rich would pay less and the middle classes would pay more.
   Passage A never mentions what middle income payers will pay, but it's implied that middle income people will pay the same since in lines 26-29 they argue that rich people will also pay about the same. The author of passage A is claiming that the new flat tax system is just as fair as the old system.
E. This is like C. It doesn't matter what legislators believe. They might be idiots.

Question 25

DISCUSSION: You're looking for something *not* in passage B. Two of the wrong answers describe arguments that passage A makes. But passage B *does* respond to those arguments, so those answers are incorrect. I'm referring to answers A and E.

A. Passage B does address a threshold, in lines 48-53.
B. This answer contradicts the passage. Passage A argues that flat taxes *are* practical. See lines 5-8.
C. Neither passage talks about investment or economic growth. These topics are relevant to taxation, but this question isn't asking you to pick something relevant in the real world. You're supposed to find things from the passages. An answer can't be right if the authors didn't talk about it.
D. CORRECT. Lines 20-26 in passage A mention this. It's the strongest part of passage A, and passage B completely fails to address it. Reducing tax evasion and tax avoidance by rich people is a major goal of tax systems.
E. Lines 30-39 in passage B address the claim that a progressive tax system is unfair.

Question 26

DISCUSSION: You're looking for something both authors disagree about. That means each passage will have a line that shows the authors have contradictory opinions.

Don't just go on memory. There are many answers that only one passage mentions. You can't assume the other author disagrees unless you actually find a line where they do disagree.

A. Both authors agree that a flat tax system can be mildly progressive, due to the exemption of a certain amount of income.
B. **CORRECT.** In lines 26-29, passage A says that the rich usually pay as much under a flat tax. In line 56, passage B says high income earners will pay less.
C. Passage B never says that flat tax systems are impossible to put into practice. So the author of passage B doesn't disagree with passage A, which says they can be put into practice.
D. Passage B describes this answer as a common myth in the first paragraph. But passage A never discusses this answer. It appears the author of passage A has not fallen prey to this myth.
E. Neither author agrees with this. Both support exemptions for some income.

Question 27

DISCUSSION: First, you need to remember the final argument of passage A. The author says that simpler tax systems encourage the rich not to evade taxes, and so the rich end up paying about as much.

As I discussed in the analysis, passage A is confusing two issues. There is a "flat" tax, and a "simplified" tax code. Their final argument is the result of a simplified tax code, but the author uses it to support a flat tax. The author of passage B can counter that a progressive tax system could be simplified without being made flat.

Most of the wrong answers are weird. C, D and E are not even things the author of passage B would agree with. We want to *support* the author of passage B!

A. This isn't a great response. It's always *possible* for people to cheat the tax system. The question is whether a flat tax system *reduces* the amount of cheating.
B. **CORRECT.** This is a complicated answer. Don't just skip complicated answers – try to understand them. This answer is saying that loopholes and deductions are the reason the rich can avoid taxes. A tax system could reduce deductions but remain progressive. The advantages described by the author of passage B come mainly from getting rid of deductions, not from flatness.
C. This is a stupid argument. Obviously, people at all levels can cheat. But it's definitely possible that rich people cheat *more*.
   Also, why would the author of passage B say this? They're arguing we should tax rich people more! They're not in the business of defending rich people.
D. So? It doesn't matter what taxpayers believe. We don't care what people believe. We care about what's true. Beliefs can be wrong.
   Also, I don't know why the author of passage B would say this. It has nothing to do with their argument.
E. This is way out of left field. The author of passage B is making an argument about income tax, and they never mention consumption taxes. So I don't know why they would bring consumption taxes up now.

Section II – Logical Reasoning

Question 1

QUESTION TYPE: Principle

CONCLUSION: You should use praise and words to train your dog.

REASONING: Treats work, but only if you have treats. You won't always have treats with you.

ANALYSIS: You have to ask yourself *why* it should matter that you won't have treats with you at all times. Use common sense.

Maybe you should only use a method you can use with your dog in all situations. That's a "principle", and it supports not using treats.

A. This tells us what people *will* do. We're looking for something that tells us what people *should* do. This isn't the only reason this answer is wrong, but this is a *very* important distinction on the LSAT and you must learn to recognize the different between what is true and what *should* be true.
(Another reason this is wrong is that we don't know if dogs learn *more* quickly with treats or with praise.)
B. This supports the idea that treat-trained dogs will obey us even if we don't have treats. This *weakens* the argument that we shouldn't use treats.
C. The stimulus never mentions whether any of the methods have "a high obedience rate in at least some circumstances". So this answer doesn't apply to anything – it's totally useless!
D. **CORRECT.** This supports the idea not to use treats. Since aren't available in all circumstances, we shouldn't use them.
E. Total nonsense. The stimulus doesn't mention any techniques that "don't work for other dogs". This answer doesn't apply to anything, and it doesn't help prove we shouldn't use treats.

Question 2

QUESTION TYPE: Weaken

CONCLUSION: Modern civilizations that rely heavily on irrigated agriculture will collapse.

REASONING: The Sumerians silted their soil with irrigation, and collapsed.

ANALYSIS: The author is assuming that what happened to the Sumerians will happen to us. The author implies that irrigation will inevitably deposit toxic salts and destroy soil.

But maybe we can learn from the Sumerians, and avoid destroying soil even if we irrigate.

A. This supports the idea that modern civilizations will collapse due to irrigation – we can't survive without it. We're trying to *weaken* the argument.
B. The Sumerians were only mentioned to show that irrigation can lead to ruin. It doesn't matter whether the Sumerians could have collapsed for other reasons – the argument is about *our* use of irrigation. The Sumerian example definitely shows that irrigation can cause problems.
C. **CORRECT.** The toxic buildup of salts and other impurities was the reason irrigation destroyed Sumerian agriculture. If our irrigation avoids this problem, then our agriculture might not collapse due to irrigation.
D. This is tempting. But look at the conclusion. It's only talking about modern civilizations that *do* use irrigation.
E. So? The point of the argument was that irrigation led to *too many* impurities in the soil. It doesn't matter if there were already some impurities. Sumerian agriculture worked for a while even as impurities were building up. It's not as if ancient Sumer instantly collapsed the moment the first impurity from irrigation entered the soil.

Question 3

QUESTION TYPE: Strengthen

CONCLUSION: It's not surprising we usually don't find dinosaur bones near dinosaur tracks in mud flats.

REASONING: Scavengers would have looked for food in mud flats.

ANALYSIS: This argument is missing something. It's a bit of a paradox: we have found dinosaur tracks and dinosaur bones, but the bones are not normally near tracks.

Why? The author says scavengers are the reason, but the author doesn't say why scavengers are important.

The question you must ask yourself is: why would scavengers prevent us finding dinosaur bones near dinosaur tracks? I didn't prephrase this one, but because I was thinking of that question, I immediately recognized the answer.

———————————

A. Who cares? We're trying to explain a fact about mud flats. It doesn't matter if dinosaur tracks are found in mountains, underwater, on the moon, etc.
B. **CORRECT.** This explains it. The dinosaur bodies were *originally* beside their tracks in mud flats. But scavengers dragged the body away from the tracks, so the bones ended up in another location.
C. This is just a fact. It doesn't explain why the bones researchers have found are not near dinosaur tracks.
D. This is like A. It's irrelevant. It doesn't matter if we found dinosaur eggs, dinosaur scales, etc. We're trying to explain the relationship between dinosaur tracks and bones. This vague reference to "other fossils" adds nothing.
E. You might have thought this meant that bones would be destroyed before they mineralized. But that's a stretch. Especially since this answer is *very* weak evidence. It just says bones take "longer" to mineralize. That could mean one second longer – you have to take LSAT answers at their weakest on strengthen questions.

Question 4

QUESTION TYPE: Identify the Conclusion

CONCLUSION: Electric stovetop burners would cause fewer fires if their max heat were limited to 350 degrees Celsius. (662 F).

REASONING: The lowest temperature that ignites cooking oil and most common fibers is 387 degrees celsius. Electric burners currently go much higher than 700 degree celsius.

ANALYSIS: You're looking for the conclusion. Ask yourself "why are they telling me this?". You're looking for a statement supported by the other statements.

Often, the first sentence is the conclusion, especially if there are no conclusion indicator words. Another sign of the conclusion is when an argument tells us what "would" happen, as the first sentence does here.

There's no infallible indicator of conclusions, but all the things above tend to indicate conclusions. Here, the author is telling us what would happen if electric stove burners were limited in heat.

———————————

A. **CORRECT.** See the analysis above. This answer is the point of the argument. The rest of the argument gives reasons why stoves would cause fewer fires if electric burners had lower max temperatures.
B. This is evidence that supports the conclusion indirectly. If 350 degrees provides enough heat, then it's realistic to limit electric stove burners to that temperature. This helps show the conclusion is not describing a ridiculous situation.
C. This is evidence that supports the conclusion that a 350 degree limit would lead to fewer fires.
D. This is evidence that supports the conclusion. Current stove max temperatures are more than high enough to start fires.
E. The argument actually doesn't say this answer. It's just implied that stoves cause fires because they go above 700 degrees celsius. That is not the main conclusion. That's something that supports the idea that we'd have fewer fires if stove heat was limited.

Question 5

QUESTION TYPE: Flawed Reasoning

CONCLUSION: Jenkins is wrong. The movie *Firepower* was intended to provoke antisocial behavior.

REASONING: The movie did produce antisocial behavior.

ANALYSIS: The author forgets that we can produce an effect even if we don't mean to. Plans backfire all the time.

If you crash your car, usually you don't *intend* to. The fact that you did crash has nothing to do with your intentions.

A. The author never said that Jenkins was biased.
   Example of flaw: Jenkins is a Democrat/ Republican. Therefore, she is wrong.
B. There's no correlation in this argument.
   Example of flaw: People who watch *Firepower* are more likely to be antisocial. Therefore, *Firepower* causes antisocial behavior.
C. This is a different flaw.
   Example of flaw: People in New York City like *Firepower*. Therefore, all Americans like *Firepower*.
D. This is tempting, but it's describing something different. The Director didn't act contrary to his expressed interest. Instead, the director's actions produced results that weren't what the director intended.
   Example of flaw: Johnson has said he plans to stop smoking. So clearly, Johnson will never smoke again. Willpower always works, right?
E. **CORRECT.** See the analysis above. The director unfortunately did cause antisocial behavior, but that doesn't mean she *intended* to do so.

Question 6

QUESTION TYPE: Principle

CONCLUSION: News reporters shouldn't use "loophole" unless they have evidence of wrongdoing.

REASONING: "Loophole" is a biased word that implies wrongdoing. News stories that use "loophole" sound like editorials.

ANALYSIS: This already seems like a good argument. That's because it likely matches your intuition for how news stories should be: unbiased.

But "unbiased" news stories are a particularly American concept. This only really emerged after the Second World War. In other places and other times, news stories often had a point of view.

You, if you are American, are applying a principle to this argument. You just have to ask yourself what this principle is. Some examples:

- News stories *shouldn't* be like editorials.
- Journalists *shouldn't* use biased words without evidence.

A. This principle helps defend those who exploit loopholes. That doesn't help. We're trying to prove what *newspaper reporters* should do.
B. This contradicts the argument. The argument implies that news stories shouldn't sound like editorials.
C. **CORRECT.** The conclusion said that reporters should not use loaded words *unless* they have evidence of bad behavior. This answer supports that. Loaded words imply wrongdoing, and this tells reporters not to imply wrongdoing without evidence.
D. The argument wasn't talking about what *editorial writers* should do. The conclusion is about what *newspaper reporters* should do. Proving editorials are right doesn't prove reporters are wrong. That's a false dichotomy.
E. The stimulus never mentions the public interest. This is playing to your biases and assumptions as an American. You might think this answer is "true", but that's not what you're looking for.

Question 7

QUESTION TYPE: Strengthen

CONCLUSION: We will definitely suffer from widespread food shortages.

REASONING: There is a maximum amount of food production possible on Earth. Population is still increasing.

ANALYSIS: This argument hasn't shown that population will increase high enough to outstrip food production. Currently, food production is increasing faster than population.

It's true that food production will max out. But to show that there will be food shortages, we need to show that population will keep increasing.

I have a bit of doubt about answer B on this argument. That's why I've made the answers longer. After thinking it over, I don't think B supports the conclusion. For instance, in the real world we are using *more* than the max capacity of the oceans right now, yet we still seem to have room to grow the food supply. So using all the fish doesn't really support the conclusion that food crises are inevitable. All it does is show that *one* potential avenue for growth of the food supply is unavailable. But there may be others.

Answer E does a better job by showing what will happen when food supply actually does max out.

Also, remember, the conclusion is not about whether we will use all the food. It's about whether we'll have food *crises* once we hit max food capacity. It's possible we'll reach our maximum production of food yet manage population in such a way that avoids famine and crisis.

A. This weakens the argument, slightly. The argument would be even stronger if food resources weren't renewable.

B. This sounds tempting, but it's not useful. Ocean food resources are already included in total food production. Our concern is whether *total* food resources will be fully utilized, not whether one part of food resources will be fully utilized. In other words, we might eat all the fish but still have plenty of wheat left to eat, and so we won't have food shortages.

Also, the argument is not necessarily talking about utilization at a given point in time. Instead, the author is asking if food resources can be *grown* in order to permit more use. Fully using fish, at given point, doesn't tell us whether growth of the food supply has become impossible. It likewise doesn't tell us that the population of humans that needs to be fed will grow past the available food supply. E does that directly, which is why it's a better answer. (Note: If E wasn't here, I would have picked B. I can see why it's not right, but there are still *some* reasons for choosing it – which is unusual.)

C. This weakens the argument. If population stops growing, we are less likely to have food shortages.

D. The argument is talking about *widespread* food shortages. Local food shortages are not the same.

E. **CORRECT.** This shows that population may continue to grow past carrying capacity. We won't stop producing more people just because we stop producing more food.

This doesn't strengthen the argument much. It's possible we wouldn't have famines even if population continued increasing briefly. Maybe we will have a food surplus and still have room for brief growth. But we only need to support the argument. We don't need to decisively prove it correct.

Question 8

QUESTION TYPE: Sufficient Assumption

CONCLUSION: New games are often less compelling because of their technical sophistication.

REASONING: It is hard for players to identify with characters they control in modern games.

ANALYSIS: On sufficient assumption questions, you have to connect the evidence to the conclusion. You "fill the gap" between premises and reasoning.

Often, on complicated questions, diagrams are useful to fill the gap. But I don't feel they're useful here. This question isn't complicated, it's just long.

The conclusion says modern games are less compelling. But none of the evidence says what makes a game compelling. All we know about games is the statement the evidence leads to: it is harder to identify with characters in modern games.

So you have to fill the gap with this premise:

Hard to identify → less compelling

A. The evidence says that in new games you *often* control a detailed figure. The conclusion is only referring to these games.
So it doesn't matter whether there are still some games with less sophisticated characters. This answer has zero impact on the argument.

B. This *weakens* the argument. We're trying to show that older games were more compelling than newer games. (i.e. newer games are less compelling)

C. All this really says is "there are other factors in making a game compelling apart from technical sophistication". That doesn't help show that technical sophistication makes games less compelling.

D. CORRECT. We know that modern, technically sophisticated characters are difficult to identify with. This answer proves that games are therefore less compelling.

E. This reverses the right answer. This tells us what happens *if* we already know a game is less compelling. But that's what we're trying to prove!

Question 9

QUESTION TYPE: Paradox

PARADOX: Pumpkins grow in areas with long, cold winters, even though these areas have a shorter growing season, and even though frost can damage pumpkins. Other, warmer regions could grow pumpkins.

ANALYSIS: There must be some reason pumpkins grow in cold regions despite the disadvantages. This paradox can only be resolved if we hear about an advantage for cold regions or a disadvantage for warm regions.

A. This makes the situation more confusing. In cold regions, frost can kill pumpkins in autumn. So the fact that pumpkins must grow till autumn puts them at risk.

B. The fact that pumpkins need bees makes the situation weirder. There will be less bee activity in cold regions.

C. This makes the situation more confusing. This says more pumpkins are sold to consumers in warm regions. So it would make sense to grow pumpkins there, close to market.

D. CORRECT. Finally. This answer gives an advantage for cold regions: the long winters kill fungus that would otherwise kill pumpkins. So pumpkins grown in warmer regions would die from this fungus even though they no risked frost damage.

E. This tells us where seeds are produced. But that doesn't necessarily have anything to do with where the seeds are *grown*. Seeds could be produced in one area and planted in another.

Question 10

QUESTION TYPE: Weaken

CONCLUSION: We should use the alternate parliamentary code.

REASONING: There are some problems with the current code. The alternate code has worked in other areas.

ANALYSIS: There are always at least three options when there are problems with a system:

1. Do nothing.
2. Fix the problems with the system.
3. Use another system.

The council chair has said we *must* do number three. They've proven number one is not a good option. But they haven't eliminated number two.

A. This doesn't matter. The stimulus already said that the way the rules have been used has been enough to weaken public confidence.
B. It doesn't matter if the alternate code has had occasional problems. The key point is that it has been used "successfully" elsewhere. That is enough.
C. **CORRECT.** See the three options above. The council member says we *must* do option 3: choose a new code. But this answer says option 2 is also a possibility: fix the current code. Fixing the problems might restore public confidence.

   Therefore, it is not true that we *must* replace the code.
D. It doesn't matter if changing codes is not *always* reasonable. Maybe this answer just means it would have been unreasonable to change the codes during World War II.
   We only care whether it's reasonable to change the codes *right now*. And the author's evidence indicates a change is reasonable: the codes have been successfully used elsewhere.
E. This strengthens the argument! This answer says the alternate code has no obvious problems.

Question 11

QUESTION TYPE: Paradox

PARADOX: Businesses use surveys to improve sales and profits. But in a recent survey of companies in a certain industry, those businesses that used surveys tended to experience a drop in profits. Businesses that didn't use surveys tended to have no drop in profits.

ANALYSIS: This argument makes a subtle shift. The first sentence is talking about businesses in general. But the study only examined a group of businesses within a single industry.

So maybe there's something about this industry that makes businesses use surveys differently or with worse results than most businesses that use surveys.

A. The stimulus never talked about any business in the study having an increase in profits. This can't explain anything.
B. This could mean that two businesses routinely use surveys ("some" can be as low as one). And we don't know whether those business had a change in profits!
   Answers that use "some" are vague, and you have to take them at their least useful.
C. **CORRECT.** This answer points out a difference between the businesses in the survey. "Most businesses" use surveys to increase profits. But this industry is different. "Most businesses in this industry" only use surveys when they get complaints.
   This explains the drop in profits. It makes sense that businesses with an increase in complaints will have less profits.
D. So? This could mean that 51% of customers answer one question slightly inaccurately. That's not necessarily significant. Customers might still answer 99% of questions correctly.
E. "Some" could mean "one business". You have to take answers that use "some" at their most useless. What one business does is not significant in this case.

Question 12

QUESTION TYPE: Necessary Assumption

CONCLUSION: We can't choose more wisely than in the past.

REASONING: Our emotional tendencies haven't changed.

ANALYSIS: On necessary assumption questions, the conclusion often has no link to the argument. On those questions, you have to assume that the conclusion depends on the reasoning. So in this case, the assumption is: "wise choices depend on emotional tendencies" or something like that.

I simplified the argument by taking out out the part about technology. Technology is just a new factor that *fails* to change anything. The main point is that new factors won't change us because we haven't changed our emotional tendencies.

A. This isn't necessary. It's only necessary that we haven't undergone any changes that would affect our capacity to choose wisely.
B. Careful. The question talked about "emotional tendencies". It didn't talk about "being in control of your emotions". You're making an assumption based on outside knowledge that our emotional tendencies lead to us not being in control of emotions, and that this is bad.
    Maybe it's actually the case that our tendencies lead us to be *extremely* in control of our emotions, but this actually prevents fully wise choices. I don't know. In any case, this answer isn't necessary. The argument never mentioned control of emotions.
C. Lessons of history? That was never in the argument. This can't be necessary.
D. Not necessary. You can negate this in such a way that it's still almost true and has no impact.
    Negation: One person, once, 1,000 years ago, made a single choice mostly based on emotions but that also included a non-emotional factor. Everyone else has chosen using emotions alone.
E. **CORRECT.** When you negate this, the argument's reasoning falls apart.
    Negation: Humans could make wiser choices even if emotional tendencies haven't changed.

Question 13

QUESTION TYPE: Role in Argument

CONCLUSION: Ornithologists say that songbirds are still threatened, even though we have begun reforestation.

REASONING: Fragmentation of forests can also harm songbirds. Open spaces make songbirds more vulnerable to predators.

ANALYSIS: Reforestation is a good thing. But ornithologists point out it's not sufficient. Reforestation is instead a useful factor that unfortunately doesn't prove the ornithologists wrong. The right answer will say the same thing, but more abstractly.

A. Not quite. It's true that various songbirds are threatened, but the fact about reforestation is actually evidence *against* this conclusion. (Though it's unfortunately not enough evidence.)
B. Nonsense. The ornithologists didn't say reforestation isn't happening. They're saying it isn't enough, because forests have too many open spaces and corridors.
C. **CORRECT.** This is it. Reforestation is useful. But it's not enough to stop songbird decline.
D. Nonsense. The stimulus didn't even talk about predator *habitats*. Instead, the passage said that open spaces make songbirds more vulnerable to predators. This is because predators can get closer to nests.
E. Ridiculous. The passage never said that predators are at risk.

Question 14

QUESTION TYPE: Flawed Reasoning

CONCLUSION: You'll be less depressed if you eat less chocolate.

REASONING: There is a correlation between chocolate and depression.

ANALYSIS: It's essential you understand why correlation doesn't lead to causation. There are always four possibilities:

1. Chocolate causes depression.
2. Depression causes chocolate eating.
3. Some third factor (e.g. stress) causes both depression and chocolate eating.
4. It's a coincidence.

We can never say that correlation leads to causation. Correlation just means two things occur together. Any of the four things above are possibilities.

A. The "improperly infers" part of this answer is right. But the rest is wrong. The argument didn't prove that chocolate "causally contributes" to depression. If chocolate did causally contribute to depression, this would be a good argument!
B. This is a different flaw.
   Example of flaw: Those with a chocolate allergy had less depression when they stopped eating chocolate. So everyone is likely to have less depression when they stop eating chocolate.
C. **CORRECT.** This describes a causation-correlation flaw. Remember, the fact that two things happen together doesn't mean that one causes the other.
D. This is a different error.
   Example of flaw: If John was planning to murder me, then John would live in the same city I do. John does live in the same city I do, so he must be planning to murder me!
E. This is a different flaw. I've actually never seen this on the LSAT, though it may exist as the correct answer on some older tests. The flaw would basically be that the conclusion is so unclear that we can't judge if it's correct. But this conclusion is very clear: less chocolate = better mood.

Question 15

QUESTION TYPE: Necessary Assumption

CONCLUSION: That journal has lots of scientific fraud.

REASONING: Many articles had images that didn't follow guidelines.

ANALYSIS: There is a difference between fraud and making a mistake. Fraud is when you intentionally try to deceive someone. It's *possible* the images were modified in order to fool people. But science is complicated. We don't know what the journal's guidelines were. It's possible the authors simply made a mistake when submitting the images.

For instance, to put an image in a scientific paper you need to copy and paste it from elsewhere. This modifies the image. You may also change the size. Maybe you make it black and white for print publication. There are all kinds of innocent modifications that might accidentally violate guidelines yet not be fraud. So the argument is assuming that the manipulations were done with fraudulent intent.

A. Verification doesn't prove anything one way or another. The scientists might have intended fraud even if they knew there were verifications, thinking they wouldn't get caught.
B. This doesn't tell us whether the images were submitted with fraud in mind. Requiring an image doesn't make an honest person fraudulent or a fraudulent person honest.
C. The negation of this doesn't affect the argument.
   Negation: Fraud can happen whether or not research has images.
D. **CORRECT.** Fraud requires intent. If you negate this then few scientists intended to commit fraud when they manipulated images. Remember, the conclusion is that fraud is a widespread problem.
   Negation: Not many (i.e. few to zero) scientists manipulated images with fraudulent intent.
E. This is not necessary.
   Negation: Widespread scientific fraud is possible in many fields, not just cellular biology.

Question 16

QUESTION TYPE: Flawed Reasoning

CONCLUSION: Contemporary artists are wrong that their works make people feel more aesthetic fulfillment.

REASONING: There are already more artworks than any human could appreciate in a lifetime.

ANALYSIS: To appreciate art, you typically have to look at it. And that requires standing in front of the painting. There is a vast amount of art available, but it is spread all over the world. In museums and in private collections. So it may be difficult for people to find aesthetic satisfaction even if in theory there is more art than anyone could ever want.

(To appreciate a great artwork, a photo usually isn't sufficient. We certainly can't assume that a great artwork is available for aesthetic fulfillment merely because it can be photographed.)

The author is not saying contemporary art is unfulfilling. Instead, they're saying that we're already at our maximum potential for fulfillment due to the great quantity of existing art. As we are at potential, contemporary art can't give us more than we already have.

———————————

A. This answer contradicts the stimulus. The author clearly said all artists believe their work can help people find aesthetic fulfillment.
B. The author didn't say that people *will* find aesthetic fulfillment. The author said they *could*.
C. The author never talked about what makes an artwork valuable.
D. **CORRECT.** This is enough to prove the argument wrong. The author said all artists are wrong. So even one artist who provides aesthetic fulfillment disproves the author. (The idea is that not everyone has access to great art, even if in theory there is more than enough art out there.)
E. This is the most tempting wrong answer. The author didn't say that contemporary works can't be fulfilling. Instead, the author said that contemporary works can't increase the *potential* for fulfillment we already have. We're already at our max potential for fulfillment due to the massive quantity of existing artworks.

Question 17

QUESTION TYPE: Most Strongly Supported

FACTS:

1. The government won't pay for Antinfia unless there are trials.
2. The maker of Antinfia won't run trials unless the government pays for the drug.

ANALYSIS: I simplified the facts slightly to make the catch-22 more obvious. The government won't pay without trials, and trials won't happen without payment. So basically, this drug isn't going to get to market. It will never undergo trials, it will never get paid for, and it will never be in widespread circulation.

Note: Catch-22 is a word that entered the English language due to Joseph Heller's novel of the same name. The main character flew on a bomber in WWII. He wanted to be declared insane so he wouldn't have to fly. But his desire to avoid flying was the proof that he was sane.

So if he wanted to fly, he would be insane, but would have to fly. If he didn't want to fly, he would be sane, therefore he must fly. There was no way out. Exactly the same situation with Antinfia.

———————————

A. Hard to say. We know the government won't pay for *Antinfia,* but maybe there are other drugs it will pay for without trials.
B. **CORRECT.** This is likely. Widespread circulation will only happen with government support. But government support won't happen without trials, which require widespread circulation. So Antinfia is stuck and will never get to market. (Technically, a rich person could fund trials, but that's ok, since this is just a "most strongly supported" question. So it's possible but very unlikely Antinfia will get to market.)
C. We have no idea what patients will do. Maybe Antinfia costs too much money even for rich people to buy it.
D. We don't know this. Antinfia is unproven, so it's unclear why the government ought to pay.
E. We don't know. The stimulus never said how much Antinfia costs. It's possible the government requires trials before funding even cheap drugs.

39

Question 18

QUESTION TYPE: Flawed Reasoning

CONCLUSION: Genetics can make you dislike vegetables.

REASONING: Volunteers who don't like vegetables have the XRV2G gene.

ANALYSIS: This is a classic LSAT error: the false comparison.

We're told that the vegetable hating group has XRV2G. But we're *not* told about the group that likes vegetables. Maybe all of them also have XRV2G! A proper comparison must tell you about *both* groups, not just one.

A. The argument didn't say this. Something can't be a flaw unless it happens. The argument just said one trait might be genetically determined. It didn't say *all* traits are.
B. This answers plays on a misunderstanding of bias and representativeness in studies.
   Let's say you do a study designed to test whether a certain drug cures cancer. And all the subjects are American. Americans are unrepresentative of humans in many ways:

   * They're richer than average
   * They live in a country that starts with 'A'
   * They watch more TV
   * They have more internet access

   All of those are unrepresentative, and none of them are relevant to the question of whether a drug cures cancer. So unrepresentativeness in one or more areas does not necessarily mean a study if flawed!
C. This means: mistaking a sufficient condition for a necessary condition. That's not what happened in this argument.
D. This possibility would strengthen the argument! It's not a flaw to overlook it. the conclusion was that genes may affect whether we like vegetables. So the more that genes affect our taste for vegetables, the better.
E. **CORRECT.** If everyone has the XRV2G gene, then it can't affect vegetable tastes.

Question 19

QUESTION TYPE: Point at Issue

ARGUMENTS: Ana argues the smoking ban is wrong because we shouldn't make laws to stop people from harming themselves.

Pankaj points out the law only covers public places. (He implies that the law is protecting others as well, from secondhand smoke. This is a warranted assumption you can make from outside knowledge.)

ANALYSIS: This question is an excellent example of how the LSAT expects you to use outside knowledge. A lot of people have the mistaken belief that you can't use outside knowledge on the LSAT. That's not true – this question *requires* you to use your knowledge that second-hand smoke is harmful.

The reason prep companies say not to use outside knowledge is because they aim their advice at low scorers. Low scorers tend to make up stuff, like "gas taxes are bad". That *might* be true, but it's a matter of controversy. You can't assume anything controversial is true. But if literally *everyone* would agree with a statement, then it is a warranted assumption from common knowledge.

A. Pankaj doesn't say whether prevention of self harm is justified. His argument implies the law is aimed at protecting people from secondhand smoke.
B. Pankaj doesn't say anything about libertarianism, so we can't know his opinion.
C. **CORRECT.** Ana agrees. Pankaj implies that he disagrees. Pankaj seems to be saying the law is aimed at protecting people from secondhand smoke, not self harm. Otherwise the law would also ban smoking in the home, not just public areas.
D. Ana doesn't say where the law bans smoking, so we can't know her opinion of this answer.
E. Ana doesn't say she opposes all regulation. She says she opposes laws against self harm. So we have no evidence she disagrees with Pankaj about this. (Pankaj clearly thinks some regulation is ok).

Question 20

QUESTION TYPE: Flawed Reasoning

CONCLUSION: Apples probably weren't cultivated in the region 5,000 years ago.

REASONING: Wild apples are smaller than the apples we grow today. 5,000 years ago, when people first started cultivating fruit, the only apples found in the region from that time were the size of wild apples.

ANALYSIS: As with question 19, outside knowledge helps you answer this question. You may know that cultivation changes foods over time. Early cultivated fruits came from wild fruits, so they would have been the same size. Then slowly over the years fruit farmers would have selected larger apples to grow.

So it wouldn't be surprising if early cultivated apples were small. There simply hadn't been enough time for them to grow.

_____

A. The conclusion was about what was true in *this* region. Other regions don't matter.
B. **CORRECT.** This is a very valid criticism. Cultivation can only change fruits over a long period of time. Every scientist and horticulturist knows this. The argument should have eliminated this possibility.
C. The argument didn't say that there are no medium sizes apples (e.g. maybe the apples fed to animals?). An answer can't be a flaw if it didn't happen.
D. This answer describes an argument that contradicts itself. That didn't happen in the stimulus.
   Example of flaw: John won't take the LSAT, therefore he won't be stressed, therefore he'll score well on the LSAT, because stress is bad for LSAT scores.
   (John can't both take and not take the LSAT)
E. This describes circular reasoning. This didn't happen in the argument.
   Example of flaw: This apple will be small because apples are small.

Question 21

QUESTION TYPE: Necessary Assumption

CONCLUSION: A happy life is a virtuous life.

REASONING: Happiness is when you have a sense of approval of your character and projects.

ANALYSIS: Generally, necessary assumption questions have a gap between evidence and reasoning. They introduce a new term in the conclusion. In this case: "a morally virtuous life". That term has no connection to the evidence. It is therefore a necessary assumption that the new term in the stimulus is related to the evidence. So this argument assumes that a morally virtuous life has something to do with approval for your projects.

Material well being is mentioned in three answers. These are traps. Material wealth has nothing to do with the argument! The author only mentioned it to clarify what the good life is. Many people think wealth is the good life, but the author says the good life is actually a moral one. This doesn't mean wealth is bad. It just means what it says: the good life is morality. Wealth might be something to seek, but by itself it isn't the determinant of a good life.

_____

A. The argument didn't say that material well being is bad. The author just mentioned it to make a distinction: the good life is morality, not wealth. This tells us what the good life is, but it doesn't necessarily mean wealth is bad.
B. **CORRECT.** The negation of this destroys the argument. The argument said happiness depends on approving of your character. If morality has nothing to do with that then there's no evidence linking morality to happiness.
   Negation: A morally virtuous life tends to have nothing to do with approving of your own character and projects.
C. This is irrelevant. The argument was talking about happiness, not pleasure.
D. Material well being isn't relevant. It was just mentioned to make a distinction: the good life means morality, not wealth.
E. Material well being doesn't matter. It was just mentioned to clarify that the good life is actually morality.

Question 22

QUESTION TYPE: Flawed Parallel Reasoning

CONCLUSION: Small farms →
Returning waste good

REASONING: returning waste good → nontoxic
AND not much energy

Small farms → nontoxic AND not much energy.

ANALYSIS: This argument make an incorrect reversal. The argument gives us *necessary* conditions for saying that returning waste is good. And we know small farms meet those necessary conditions.

But you can never prove something with necessary conditions. To prove that returning waste is good, we would need a *sufficient* condition. And the argument hasn't given us a sufficient condition.

The conclusion reverses the evidence and assumes that anything that meets the two conditions is good. So we're looking for an argument:

- A conditional statement
- A situation that meets the necessary conditions
- An incorrect reversal of the statement

A. This is a good argument. The conditional statement gives a sufficient condition for thriving, and greenhouses meet that condition.
B. This is a good argument. It provides a sufficient condition.
C. **CORRECT.** This matches. We have necessary conditions for viability. The argument reverses this and assumes they are sufficient conditions.
D. This is a good argument. It gives a set of sufficient (and necessary) conditions, so meeting the conditions proves the conclusion.
E. This is a bad argument. It would be good if it showed the meal had no carbohydrates and protein. But this argument didn't do that – the 20% remainder of the meal might have had both carbs and protein.
   This is failure to meet a condition. It's not an incorrect reversal, which was the error in the argument.

Question 23

QUESTION TYPE: Strengthen

CONCLUSION: Phenazines bring nutrients to bacteria in the interior of the colony.

REASONING: No evidence is given for the hypothesis.

ANALYSIS: To answer this, you must imagine a colony of bacteria. The question says "interior bacteria". So presumably some parts of the colony are in touch with the outside environment, and some aren't.

The right answer is creative. I couldn't have prephrased it. But I saw it supported the idea that interior bacteria couldn't get nutrients without phenazines.

A. **CORRECT.** Think about it. If interior bacteria need phenazines for nutrients, what will happen without phenazines? The interior bacteria will suffer. So this wrinkled shape is a response. It puts more interior bacteria in direct contact with the outside.
   If phenazines are present, then it seems wrinkling is not required, because the phenazines send nutrients directly inside.
B. This answer has nothing to do with nutrients.
C. This is a false comparison. We don't know what happens to colonies in nutrient-poor soil. The answers *implies* that they will grow less quickly without phenazines, but that's not something we can assume – we need a direct comparison.
D. This answer is about how well bacteria can fend off other bacteria. The hypothesis was about phenazines and interior nutrition, not about how phenazines help fend off other bacteria.
E. This doesn't help the argument. The hypothesis is that phenazines help interior bacteria! It's not useful to learn that interior bacteria die faster than outer bacteria.
   (Technically, this is a false comparison. It's useless information. We don't know if interior bacteria are also more likely to die without phenazines.)

Question 24

QUESTION TYPE: Must be True

FACTS:

1. Widely acknowledge (most) → restore
2. Authenticity suspect SOME restore
3. Restore → Safety ensured
4. ~~Frequently consulted → restore~~
   Contrapositive: restore → frequently consulted

Combined statements:

Widely acknowledged (most) → Restore → Safety ensured AND frequently consulted

Authenticity suspect SOME restore → Safety ensured AND frequently consulted

Contrapositive:

(Note: You can't take contrapositives of "some" and "most" statements. You can only take contrapositives of conditional statements)

~~Safety ensure~~ OR ~~frequently consulted~~ → ~~restore~~

ANALYSIS: This question relies heavily on conditional reasoning. This is an excellent question to redo in order to master conditional reasoning. It has:

- Taking the contrapositive of a conditional and combining it with another statement
- Combining conditional statements to get multiple necessary conditions for a single sufficient condition
- Combining a "most" statement with a conditional
- Combining a "some" statement with a conditional

I'm going to take this opportunity to give a full explanation of how to combine "some" and "most" statements with conditional statements. This is a large topic that appears maybe once every LSAT. I'm explaining it in full here because I've never seen a question that illustrates this so completely. I'm going to use an abstract example to explain, with the letters Z, A, B and C. This is because "some" statements and conditionals are rather mathematical, and you should learn to look at them structurally, no matter what the subject is.

Note that this example with Z, A, B and C *exactly* parallels this combined statement from the question:

"Authenticity suspect SOME restore → Safety ensured AND frequently consulted"

So if you aren't sure how I created that, follow along with the abstract example, and replace Z with "authenticity suspect" etc. Here are our facts:

Z some A
A → B
A → C

So I've given two necessary conditions for A, and I've also said some Z's are A. First, we want to simplify the conditional statements with A. You can combine them, like this. There's no sense keeping two separate statements:

A → B and C

This matches the combined conditional statement I made for the stimulus. By the way, a "conditional" statement is just a statement with sufficient and necessary conditions.

Next, "some" statements (and "most" statements) can combine with *sufficient* conditions. In other words, if a statement said "B some Q", I couldn't do anything with it, because B is a necessary condition. But since A is a *sufficient* condition, I can combine "Z some A" with it.

Z some A → B and C

(Note: If I had said "A some Z", I could do the same thing, since "some" statements are reversible.)

This matches the "some" + conditional statement I made earlier, for the stimulus (A = restore, etc.)

Let's talk about what it means. This means that if something is A, it's always B and C. And if something is not C or not B, it's not A.

That's the conditional statement and its contrapositive, and most people know that. It's the "some" part that's different.

We don't know how many Z's there are, or A's, or B's. There could be only one Z and 10,000,000 B's, or 10,000,000 Z's and all of them are B's.

Let's say there is one Z (maybe not the only one). This Z is named Zogbert. What do we know about Zogbert?

- She's an A.
- Because she's an A, she's also a B.
- Because she's an A, she's also a C.

So Zogbert is a Z, A, B and C. If someone says "some Z's are C" then that's a true statement. It applies to Zogbert, at the very least.

We *can* go backwards and say "some B's are Z". Again, this applies to Zogbert, since she is a Z and a B. But we have no idea if many B's are Z or if many Z's are B. We only know about Zogbert and the other "some" Z's that are A's.

Going back to the stimulus, I could say this: "Some manuscripts with their authenticity suspect are frequently consulted."

(This combines the first part of the "some" statement with one of the necessary conditions of "restore")

You can always combine a "some" or a "most" statement with the left-hand side of a conditional statement, which I've done above.

Hopefully "some" is clearer now. It's a little abstract, but this abstract structure occurs on dozens of LSAT questions, including this one, so make sure you understand it.

Let's apply this to the original statements. Suppose there's a document called the Odessa Palimpsest (I made that up). It's going to be restored. All documents that will be restored are frequently consulted and have their safety ensured. So we can say of the Odessa Palimpsest:

- It will be restored.
- Its safety will be ensured.
- It is frequently consulted.

You can also go backwards and say "some" documents with safety ensured will be restored (i.e. the Odessa Palimpsest)

We *can't* say the Odessa Palimpsest is widely acknowledged to be important or has its authenticity suspect. That's because you can't go backwards and say a specific document has the "some" or "most" statements apply to it.

The "most" and "some" statements only let me make general claims about a group. I can't know if an individual item falls into those groups unless I'm told. It's a question of quantity.

This is why you can't go backwards with "most" statements. We saw this statement in the stimulus:

Widely acknowledged (most) → Restore → Safety ensured AND frequently consulted

There might only be 11 documents in the collection that have widely acknowledged significance. "Most" of them would be 6.

We can say that those 6 documents will be restored, and that their safety can be ensured, and that they are frequently consulted. So far, this is exactly what you can do with "some" statements.

But you can't go backwards and say that "most documents with safety ensured" have widely acknowledged significance. That's because there could be 10,000 documents with safely ensured. So when going backwards with a "most" statement, you can only say things like "some documents with their safety ensured have widely acknowledged significance". This last statement refers to those 6 documents that are "most" of the documents with widely acknowledged significance.

Phew. If this is the first time you've seen this kind of discussion of "some" and "most" combined with conditionals, I'm sure that was confusing. Refer back to this explanation often. And play around with "some" and "most". Make up some examples that are true in real life, and see how they work.

For example, suppose you have three sisters. You can say "most of my family are women, and all women have legs". You can go backwards to say "some people with legs are in my family". But you can't go backwards to say "most people with legs are in my family". That's just silly. All of these things the LSAT talks about are real. You can use real life examples to see what's correct.

_____

A. CORRECT. This follows from reading the "some" statement + the conditional statement left-to-right. You can combine the "some" statement with both necessary conditions. So, some documents with authenticity suspect:

* Will be restored
* Are frequently consulted
* Have their safety ensured

We know the latter two points are true because they're true of *any* documents that are restored. And some documents with authenticity suspect will be restored.

B. This isn't true. We only know we're restoring "most" documents of widely acknowledged cultural significance. It's possible some won't be restored, maybe because their safety can't be ensured.

C. This is an incorrect reversal of the statement about safety. Everything restored can be restored safely. But it's possible that some things that can be restored safely nonetheless won't be restored.

D. The stimulus never mentioned "most susceptible to deterioration". This can't possibly be the right answer.

E. We don't know. We know that "most" documents widely acknowledged to be significant will be restored. That might mean they're all restored, or it might mean some won't be. We don't know why some won't be restored. It COULD be because they're not consulted, but it could also be for some other reason – perhaps they can't be restored safely, or they fail to meet another necessary condition for restoration. (There could be other necessary conditions we don't know about).

Question 25

QUESTION TYPE: Strengthen

CONCLUSION: It is wrong to say that direct mail advertising is bad for the environment.

REASONING: If people buy using direct mail, they don't have to drive to the store.

ANALYSIS: I don't get many direct mail ads. The last one I got was for a pen with my business name on it. They actually mailed me a sample pen.

Needless to say, I've never had a desire for a pen with "LSAT Hacks" on it. If someone gave me free LSAT Hacks pens, I believe I would get rid of them, unless they happened to be *really* nice pens.

So this direct mail ad was nothing but bad for the environment. It wasted paper. It wasted gas in the postal delivery system. And if I had responded to it, it would have been a waste of the pens I would otherwise never have bought.

We can strengthen the argument by saying direct mail ads are not like this. That instead, we only get direct mail ads for things we would otherwise drive to the store to buy. If you buy toilet paper from a direct mail ad rather than driving, then you probably are helping the environment, slightly.

A. This *weakens* the argument by showing that direct mail ads can lead to driving.

B. CORRECT. This strengthens the argument. If you buy direct mail, you don't have to drive. So if you were already going to buy the products you bought via direct mail, then it saved you a trip.

C. Hard to say how this helps. Whether you buy from direct mail or a magazine, you're not driving to the store. This answer should have compared direct mail to ads that require you to go to the store.

D. This shows that direct mail advertisers aren't idiots. They target their ads. But this doesn't prove the ads reduce driving.

E. This shows direct mail is growing. But that doesn't help show that direct mail is reducing in-store purchases. Maybe direct mail just makes people buy more overall.

Question 26

QUESTION TYPE: Parallel Reasoning

CONCLUSION: New country (most) → ~~monarch~~

REASONING: Country (most) → ~~monarch~~

Older countries are more likely to be ruled by monarchs.

ANALYSIS: Note: "likely" is a synonym for "most" on the LSAT. Same goes for usually, tends to, probably, etc.

This is a good argument. We know any given country is unlikely to be ruled by a monarch, since most countries are not ruled by monarchs. So we could *already* say that a new country is unlikely to be ruled by a monarch (because this is true for *any* country).

Then the argument makes this even more certain by saying that new countries are even less likely to be ruled by monarchs. We already knew that countries in general are unlikely to be ruled by monarch, so making a set of countries *less* likely to be ruled by monarchs strengthens this conclusion.

To match this structure, we should have a conclusion that's already true for the group as a whole, and then make that conclusion even more true for a subset by saying that subset is even more likely to match the conclusion.

The answers all have the same subject matter: novels and movies. The wrong answers tend to switch terms. In the stimulus, the evidence and conclusion were all statements about countries. In the wrong answers, the statements often switch from novels to movies.

A. This is wrong because the evidence is about what's likely for a novel, but the conclusion is about what's likely for a movie.

B. This answer switches from talking about novels, to talking about movies, then back to novels.

C. This has two differences. First, the second sentence should have said "the less popular a novel is, the less likely it will be made into a movie". And the conclusion should have been that therefore unpopular novels are probably not made into movies.

In other words, this answer should have been phrased like answer D.

D. CORRECT. This matches. Every statement is about novels. We already know a novel is unlikely to be made into a movie, because most aren't. The conclusion is about a subset of novels: unpopular ones. We know these are even less likely to be made into movies, so it's especially true that they're unlikely to be made into movies.

E. This conclusion is a sort of incorrect reversal. We know that novels with simple plots are *more likely* to be made into movies. But that doesn't mean they're likely to be made into movies. Maybe they only have a 2% chance, while most novels have an even lower chance, 1%.

Section III – Logical Reasoning

Question 1

QUESTION TYPE: Paradox

PARADOX: You should brush your teeth after every meal to remove sugar. Sugars cause cavities. Yet if you can't brush your teeth, you should chew gum, even if it contains sugar. This will reduce cavities.

ANALYSIS: Gum reduces cavities, *even though* it contains sugar, which increases cavities. So there must be something the gum does that reduces cavities even more than sugar increases them.

It's possible gum is good even though it has *one* bad effect (sugar). We tend to forget that something can be good even if it has flawed.
Don't be a perfectionist.

Two of the answers just show why gum is *not bad*. Remember, you're trying to prove that gum is *good*. "Not bad" and "good" are not the same thing. One answer talks about improved oral health. But the conclusion is specifically about cavities.

––––––––––––––––

A. This doesn't explain why gum is *good*. At best, a lower sugar content explains why gum is less bad. The dentist wouldn't tell you to eat plain sugar to cure cavities, even if the amount was small. Sugar, by itself, is harmful.
B. This answer isn't helpful. It doesn't tell us why chewing gum can prevent cavities. It just tells us we can fix some cavities.
C. **CORRECT.** The stimulus said cavities happen when enamel is demineralized. Chewing gum remineralizes enamel.

   So gum protects teeth, even though *one part* of gum (sugar) harms teeth.
D. This tells us that gum isn't necessarily harmful. As long as you brush your teeth within 24 hours, you should be ok. But this answer doesn't tell us why gum is *helpful*.
E. This is tempting. But the conclusion is that gum will *reduce cavities*. This answer talks about contributing to the health of the oral tract. That's too broad. We need to show gum helps cavities.

Question 2

QUESTION TYPE: Weaken

CONCLUSION: The discovery of a primitive land mammal in New Zealand (NZ) disproves the idea that NZ birds flourished due to a lack of mammals.

REASONING: Until the discovery, there were no known land mammals in New Zealand. Now we've discovered NZ once had at least one native land mammal.

ANALYSIS: This is a subtle question. You have to read carefully to see what the opposing theory is:

"New Zealand birds did well because they did not face competition from land mammals"

To disprove the theory, we'd have to show there *was* competition from mammals. This argument hasn't done that. It's just shown that one mammal used to exist in New Zealand. It's possible the animal didn't provide competition.

––––––––––––––––

A. This *strengthens* the argument. The more land mammals existed in New Zealand, the more likely they were to compete with birds.
B. **CORRECT.** This ruins the argument. If the land mammal was extinct before birds arrived in NZ, then the mammal couldn't have competed with birds.
C. This answer is irrelevant. Introducing reptiles doesn't help show that birds faced no competition from mammals. We don't even know if this discovery is significant – maybe scientists already knew New Zealand had reptiles and insects.
D. This was a tempting answer – it seems to show that mammals do destroy bird populations. But notice that it's talking about countries with a "rich and varied" mammal population. We only have evidence that New Zealand had *one* mammal. That's hardly rich and varied. This answer doesn't fit with our evidence.
E. This answer slightly strengthens the argument by showing it's possible we were mistaken about New Zealand's lack of mammals.

47

Question 3

QUESTION TYPE: Identify the Conclusion

CONCLUSION: The newspaper reporter is not a true restaurant critic.

REASONING: The reporter has said he has no expertise about food or food preparation. His past experience was as a political reporter.

ANALYSIS: On identify the conclusion questions, ask yourself: "Why are they telling me this?"

The restaurant owner is annoyed at the negative review. So she's trying to show that the review shouldn't be listened to. She wants to show us that the newspaper reporter isn't really a good critic.

Notice the word "but". Words like "but", "however" etc. almost always introduce a conclusion.

The real point of the argument, of course, is that we should not pay attention to the negative review. But that main point is merely implied. The fact about the reporter not being a true critic is the explicitly stated conclusion.

A. This is evidence that supports the conclusion that the reporter is not a true food critic.
B. This is evidence that the reporter has no background in food and thus they are not a true food critic.
C. The fact that the reporter is a good writer is evidence in favor of the reporter. The restaurant owner hopes to sound more persuasive by acknowledging a positive (but mostly irrelevant) fact about the reporter.
D. **CORRECT.** This is the conclusion. The word "but" indicates that this is the author's opinion. And this answers the question "why is the owner telling us this?". The entire argument was aimed at convincing us that the reporter is not a true food critic (and therefore we shouldn't pay attention to the negative review).
E. This is an analogy that supports the conclusion that someone without food training is not a food critic.

Question 4

QUESTION TYPE: Necessary Assumption

CONCLUSION: The hypothesis that our solar system formed from a supernova is wrong.

REASONING: If we formed from a supernova, iron-60 would have been around in the early years of our solar system. But we didn't find iron-60 in meteorites that formed in the early years of our solar system.

ANALYSIS: The stimulus said there would have been iron-60 present in the early solar system. So we can say "no iron-60 → no supernova"

But the argument gives different evidence. The argument didn't say there *was no* iron-60. It says we didn't *find* iron-60, in a *meteorite*. There are two flaws:

1. Maybe iron-60 existed, but we just failed to find it.
2. Maybe iron-60 could have existed even if it didn't leave traces in meteorites.

A. This *weakens* the argument. It shows that meteorites don't give us a good view of what was in supernovas.
   Negation: Meteorites contain exact what was produced by supernovas.
B. Who cares about other solar systems? We're talking about *our own* solar system.
C. Who cares about other forms of iron? The evidence is only about iron-60.
D. This isn't relevant. The stimulus says that a supernova would have led to iron-60 *early* in the solar system's history. Meteorites that formed late in the solar systems history can't tell us about the early history of the solar system. Maybe the iron-60 in those meteorites only appeared in the later years of the solar system.
E. **CORRECT.** This is essential to the argument. If you negate it, then it's possible that iron-60 existed in the early years of the solar system, even though we didn't find it.
   Negation: We might not have found iron-60 in the meteorites, even if there had been iron-60 in the early years of the solar system.

Question 5

QUESTION TYPE: Paradox

PARADOX: Carbon monoxide disguises the color of tuna. Carbon monoxide can't hurt people. Yet more people will get sick from tuna that is treated with carbon monoxide.

ANALYSIS: Think broadly. When tuna is treated with carbon monoxide, two things happen:

1. The tuna has carbon monoxide on it.
2. The tuna won't turn brown with age.

Our instinct is to suspect the first reason. Eww, chemicals. But the argument specifically rules out direct harm from carbon monoxide.

So it must be the second reason that harms people. There's really no other possibility – color is the cause. I didn't prephrase the precise answer, but I was looking for something to do with color.

Remember, your job is to explain why carbon monoxide seems to be causing harm even though it can't cause harm directly. Most of the wrong answers just tell us random facts about tuna. On paradox questions, you always have to ask yourself if an answer *explains* the situation.

A. The stimulus was about people who *eat* tuna. Workers in tuna plants aren't relevant.
B. This is just a random fact about how much tuna we eat. This doesn't tell us why carbon monoxide seems to be causing harm.
C. **CORRECT.** This clears things up. Carbon monoxide causes no direct harm. But it hides evidence that tuna has gone bad. And if you eat spoiled tuna, you can get very sick.
D. This is just a random fact. This doesn't tell us *why* carbon monoxide seems to be making people sick even though it's supposed to be safe.
E. This tells us why manufacturers use carbon monoxide. It doesn't tell us why carbon monoxide seems to cause harm.

Question 6

QUESTION TYPE: Strengthen

CONCLUSION: "Short" and "long" descriptive labels for gamma ray bursts are no longer useful.

REASONING: "Short" and "long" describe gamma ray bursts. Short and long refer to how long the bursts last. Recently, we found a burst that lasted a long time but otherwise was similar to a short burst.

ANALYSIS: This is a confusing situation. I had to read it a few times to figure out what it means. I'm going to make up a description of long and short gamma bursts to illustrate. Typical features:

Long: Lasts a long time, smells smoky, looks purple, sounds loud

Short: Last a short time, smells like oranges, looks green, sounds like a whispered voice

Obviously, these are nonsense descriptions, but let's go with it. The question is whether these long and short labels are useful, or whether we should replace them with something like "type A" and "type B".

Recent burst: Lasts a long time, smells like oranges, looks green, sounds like a whispered voice

How do we classify this burst? It is "most similar" to a short burst. But the length matches a long burst. We actually don't know the proper way to classify bursts. But we are supposed to strengthen the argument that "short" and "long" are not good labels. We can do this by showing that it's the other qualities that matter for classification, not length.

If classification is mostly based on length, then calling the bursts "long" and "short" also makes sense. But if classification is based on the other factors, then we should call the recent burst "short". But that's misleading, because the burst lasted a long time. "Type B" would be clearer.

Note: the question stem uses the words "most strongly supported". But if you look at what the full stem *means,* this is clearly a "strengthen" question.

A. This *weakens* the argument. The point of mentioning the unusual gamma burst was to show that the classification system doesn't work for all gamma bursts. But if only *one* gamma burst doesn't fit into the system, then maybe we can safely keep the current system. One exception isn't a big deal.

B. This may *weaken* the argument. The whole point of the unusual gamma burst is that duration is *not* a good way to categorize. The unusual burst was long, but otherwise resembled a short burst. If length is good enough on its own, then maybe we don't have to worry that the recent burst otherwise resembled a short burst.

C. **CORRECT.** This shows that we should probably classify the recent gamma burst as "short", even though it lasted a long time. Therefore, the label "short" is misleading, and we should replace it with something like "type B".

D. This is totally irrelevant. We don't know what cosmic factors create gamma bursts, so we don't know if the astrophysicist thinks gamma bursts should be categorized by cosmic event. The author never said that cosmic events were relevant.

E. This talks about whether we *can* replace descriptive labels. But the argument wasn't about that. Instead, the argument was about whether descriptive labels were still useful.

Something might be deeply flawed, but impossible to replace.

Question 7

QUESTION TYPE: Flawed Reasoning

CONCLUSION: Those with a greater tendency to laugh will have faster immune system recovery. Even if they laugh just a little.

REASONING: Those with a greater tendency to laugh had greater immune system recovery after they watched comic videos.

ANALYSIS: This question drowns you in words. The test writers wanted to hide an obvious error: the stimulus doesn't tell you how much each group laughs!

We know this: two groups watched comic videos. And those who tended to laugh more had better recovery. The evidence does say "this indicates" laughter can help, so we know it's true.

But the stimulus left out a key detail. How much does each group laugh? The conclusion implies that the group with a greater tendency to laugh didn't laugh as much. But the evidence didn't say that! Maybe those who tend to laugh, laughed *more* at the comic videos, and this is why they recovered faster.

A. **CORRECT.** Exactly. The evidence never says how much each group laughed at the videos. We would normally expect the group with a greater tendency to laugh to laugh more.

B. The stimulus was talking about *gains* in immune system strength. Starting strength isn't relevant – we only care how much the immune systems of each group *improved*.

C. Look carefully at the conclusion. It's not talking about the whole population. It's just talking about patients in hospitals who need to recover from illness.

D. The stimulus said one group had a greater tendency to laugh "to begin with". So immune system strength gains didn't cause this difference. It was already there, and the group that had a tendency to laugh saw a more rapid recovery of immune system strength.

E. The stimulus is talking about immune system recovery. This *helps* recover from illness, but the immune system is the main point.

Question 8

QUESTION TYPE: Strengthen

CONCLUSION: The study shows that male guppies will alter their courting behavior based on feedback from females.

REASONING: Females liked orange, and male guppies tended to show their orange side.

ANALYSIS: This argument is missing a step. It's not clear how feedback from the females made the males decide to show their orange side. Maybe male guppies are hardwired to show their orange side, no matter what the females do.

Females *could* have influenced males. We can strengthen the argument by showing they definitely did.

A. CORRECT. A model of a female guppy can't give feedback – it's not alive. This answer shows that, absent feedback, males are not more likely to show orange. That means that with the live females, it's likely that males showed their orange side *because* they got feedback from females.

B. We don't care about other species. That information can't tell us anything about guppies.

C. We don't care which guppies succeed in reproducing. The conclusion was very specific. It's about whether female feedback can alter male *courting behavior.*

D. It doesn't matter what color females are. The point was that males have a choice of colors to show females. We want to prove that females influenced this choice.

E. This weakens the argument. If guppies can't interact, then there's less possibility for feedback. This makes it *less* likely that feedback from females caused males to show their orange sides.

Question 9

QUESTION TYPE: Identify the Conclusion

CONCLUSION: It would be dangerous to unilaterally get rid of nuclear weapons.

REASONING: Some countries with nuclear weapons may soon be in civil war. They can't be trusted to obey international agreements.

ANALYSIS: The argument has the following structure:

1. Opposing opinion ("some proponents")
2. Conclusion ("this would be dangerous")
3. First premise ("because....")
4. Second premise ("These countries cannot be relied upon....")

The word "because" indicates the conclusion. In an argument, the words before "because" are usually the conclusion, and what comes after "because" is evidence.

Also, usually when an answer says "some proponents argue", the author's conclusion will be "those proponents are wrong". This is a very common LSAT structure and you must learn to recognize it.

A. This is evidence. The conclusion is that, *because of this,* we shouldn't get rid of our nuclear weapons.

B. The author *disagrees* with this idea. Countries in civil war wouldn't be influenced by international agreements.

C. The author doesn't say this. This answer is playing on your outside knowledge. In the real world, many countries hide the extent of their nuclear programs. But while this is *true,* it has nothing to do with the argument!

D. The author didn't say we couldn't make an agreement. We might succeed in making an international agreement. But it would be dangerous to rely on it, since countries in civil war can't be expected to obey the agreement.

E. CORRECT. This is it. It would be risky *because* many countries are near civil war and couldn't be relied upon.

Question 10

QUESTION TYPE: Weaken

CONCLUSION: If you fall or bump your head, you should take the whiplash treatment course.

REASONING: It's *possible* for falls or bumps on the head to cause whiplash.

ANALYSIS: In real life, something can *sometimes* be a cause, without *always* being a cause. Many people forget this on the LSAT. If they see something can be a cause, they assume it always is. This is because they've learned conditional reasoning and assume that every cause is a sufficient cause.

The LSAC noticed this trend, and so they've started making questions that test your ability to spot that something can occasionally be a cause without always being a cause.

In this case, the argument is flawed because the advertisement hasn't shown that every fall or bump leads to whiplash. If many falls and bumps don't lead to whiplash then there's no reason to take the whiplash course after every fall.

A. This is tempting, but notice that the conclusion doesn't say you should take the whiplash course when you're shoved from behind. Shoves from behind were just mentioned for emphasis, but they're not structurally part of the argument.

B. This mixes together two terms from the stimulus. It's irrelevant. The conclusion was that you should *always* go to the whiplash course after a fall. It shouldn't matter if the fall was due to a car crash or just due to clumsiness while walking.

C. This isn't relevant. The conclusion is about what to do if you fall, or if you bump your head. The fact that whiplash also has other causes doesn't tell us anything about falls.

D. **CORRECT.** The argument said falling *can* cause whiplash. This answer points out that while this is true, falling *rarely* causes whiplash. It doesn't make sense to take a whiplash treatment course after falls that don't cause whiplash.

E. This *strengthens* the argument. No matter the cause of your whiplash, the whiplash course should be relevant.

Question 11

QUESTION TYPE: Flawed Reasoning

CONCLUSION: We should develop the trail.

REASONING: One group that opposes the trail has a bad argument.

ANALYSIS: The author's argument against the citizen's group is actually pretty good. If most trail users will care for nature, then it doesn't sound like littering is a big worry.

But that doesn't prove we *should* develop the trail. There might be other reasons not to develop. Maybe the trail will be too costly to maintain. Maybe not many people will use it. Maybe we'll put a train line back in someday.

You can't say that a conclusion is true just because a criticism of the conclusion is wrong.

A. **CORRECT.** The author hasn't given *any* evidence for why we *should* build the trail. They've just shown that one argument for why *not* to build the trail is flawed.

B. This is a different error.
Example of flaw: No individual hiker can harm nature. So the whole group of hikers can't harm nature.

C. This is a different flaw: circular reasoning.
Example of flaw: It's a good idea to develop the trail, because trail development is good.

D. This is a different flaw. The author gave evidence about a majority, not about a few.

E. This is a different flaw: an ad hominem attack.
Example of flaw: A citizen's group opposes the trail. But they smell bad. So we shouldn't listen to them.

Question 12

QUESTION TYPE: Strengthen

CONCLUSION: There is no imminent shortage of engineers.

REASONING: Engineering and science salaries have stayed stable; they aren't increasing. Unemployment is the same as in other fields.

ANALYSIS: This is a simple argument, but it's worded strangely. It took me a while to understand it. The conclusion is that we have enough engineers and scientists. Here are the two reasons, in plainer English:

1. If we had a shortage, engineering salaries would be increasing. But salaries aren't increasing.
2. If we had a shortage, unemployment would be low. But unemployment is normal. That means we have enough scientists and engineers.

Take hard sentences part by part. For instance: "There is little upward pressure on the salaries of scientists and engineers". The "salaries of scientists and engineers" is how much we pay them. If there were "upward pressure", that would mean we're paying them more. Meaning there is a shortage. Instead, there is no upward pressure. Therefore there is no shortage.

This is already a good argument. Make it stronger by showing another reason why we won't have a catastrophic shortage of scientists and engineers.

A. This doesn't matter. The question is about the number of scientists all across society.

B. This was tempting, but I don't know why. It's just something that's obviously true. It doesn't help show there are enough engineers. Almost any profession has "some chance of financial success"; this doesn't tell us people will be flooding into engineering.

C. CORRECT. University students from the past five years will soon be entering the profession. So we currently have no shortage, *and* this answer tells us there's a ready supply of new scientists and engineers in the pipeline.

D. This is just fluff. The argument is talking about undersupply in the scientific market in general. This answer doesn't tell us what's happening in the overall scientific market.

E. This *weakens* the argument. If skills must be kept current, then it is *harder* to keep up the supply of engineers.

Question 13

QUESTION TYPE: Principle – Strengthen

ARGUMENTS: Rhonda says you should help people, because you'll have a richer life.

Brad says you should help your friends and relatives, because they'll be most likely to help you later.

ANALYSIS: Both Rhonda and Brad are selfish – they give to get. They both suggest helping others, but only because you'll benefit from the help you gave.

We want to strengthen both arguments, so the right answer says we should do things that help ourselves.

A. This doesn't support Brad's argument. He's arguing we should only help a limited number of people: friends and family.
B. This is totally irrelevant to both arguments. It says, for example, that if you expect someone to be an asshole, then you should be mean to them. Rhonda never says you should be mean to anyone. You should help others.
   And Brad isn't talking about how to treat everyone. He's talking about who you should help.
C. **CORRECT.** This supports both arguments. Rhonda says you'll have a richer life by helping others. Brad says that helping friends and family will gain you favors later. So both of them suggest helping yourself, ultimately.
D. This doesn't support Rhonda. She doesn't say why those who help others have richer lives. Maybe it's just because altruism makes them feel good, even if no one returns their favors.
E. Neither author talks about taking pride in helping people. This is totally irrelevant.

Question 14

QUESTION TYPE: Flawed Reasoning

CONCLUSION: We shouldn't hide cable TV lines underground.

REASONING: Some animals will still get electrocuted even if we hide cable TV lines underground.

ANALYSIS: You may have heard the expression "Don't let the perfect be the enemy of the good". That's the error the columnist makes.

It sounds like the environmentalists' proposal is *better* than what we're doing now. So we should probably do it. The columnist hasn't given good evidence. He's just shown the proposal is not *perfect*. That's not good enough. He ought to show that it's *worse* than what we're doing now.

A. This is a different flaw. The argument didn't reverse any sufficient-necessary statements.
   Example of flaw: If the plan would kill all the animals, then it would be a bad plan.
   This plan doesn't kill *all* the animals, so it's not a bad plan.
B. **CORRECT.** A proposal can be useful even if it's not a perfect solution. For instance, I doubt studying will get you a perfect 180 on the LSAT. But that doesn't mean studying isn't useful.
C. I can see how you'd think this was the answer. The author did judge based only on one factor. But the author did not incorrectly exclude other factors. This answer would only apply if there was an additional factor that demanded consideration, or if the author stated, without evidence, that there were no other factors.
D. This is a different flaw: an ad hominem flaw.
   Example of flaw: The environmentalists made a proposal. But they're lazy hippies, so I'm not going to listen to them.
E. This is a different flaw.
   Example of flaw: Plan B would save all the animals, and earn us $10 billion dollars per year.

   But we shouldn't do plan B, because plan A already works. Plan A saves 75% of animals.

Question 15

QUESTION TYPE: Role in Argument

CONCLUSION: *Thrinaxodon* was probably warm blooded.

REASONING: *Thrinaxodon* may have had whiskers. If it had whiskers, it would have had other hair. The other hair would have provided insulation. This insulation would only be useful for a warm blooded animal.

ANALYSIS: The question is asking about the second sentence. This is a premise. Don't be fooled by the word "clearly". This can indicate a conclusion, but here it's just part of a conditional statement:

Whiskers → Other hair

In fact, you can make a longer chain:

Whiskers → Other hair → Insulation → Insulation not useful for cold blooded

We think *Thrinaxodon* probably had whiskers. Hence it probably was warm blooded. The second sentence is a premise that supports this conclusion.

A. This answer is part right, but misstates the conclusion. The conclusion is after "therefore" – the *Thrinaxodon* was probably warm blooded.
B. **CORRECT.** The conclusion is after "therefore". Everything else in the argument is a premise that supports the conclusion.
C. The line in question is just a premise. It's true the sentence said "clearly". But that doesn't always indicate a conclusion. In this case it's just part of a conditional statement. It's like saying "clearly, all cats have tails". "Cat" is a sufficient condition.
D. Right after this sentence, the argument says "therefore". That means the argument *agrees* with the sentence in question, and uses it as evidence for the conclusion.
E. There is no phenomenon in the conclusion. A "phenomenon" is a fact. The author claims that *Thrinaxodon* was probably warm blooded. That is a hypothesis, not a fact. Also the sentence in question definitely supports the hypothesis in the conclusion.

Question 16

QUESTION TYPE: Complete the Argument

CONCLUSION: Those governments should tax consumption.

REASONING: Taxing consumption would improve savings. It's necessary to improve savings.

ANALYSIS: The author is making a subtle argument. They are not saying that income taxes are always bad. They are saying countries should not *primarily* use income taxes, especially if those countries are trying to increase savings.

So those countries that rely primarily on income taxes and need to raise savings should tax consumption more and income less.

A. The argument never talks about taxes on savings and investment. Maybe governments *don't* tax savings. It doesn't make sense to conclude with this answer unless we know savings are actually being taxed.
B. This is too strong. The argument said that improving savings is a *necessary* condition. So we have no evidence that the author thinks economies would "rapidly improve" with better tax policies.
C. The author doesn't say that governments should use *only* consumption taxes. There argument is just we should tax consumption more and income less.
D. **CORRECT.** This is an appropriately subtle conclusion. The author said the problem is that countries rely "primarily" on income taxes. The author is not categorical, so it sounds like their main point is that we should have *more* consumption taxes and *less* income taxes.
E. Too strong. The author said "many countries" rely *primarily* on income taxes. There may be some countries that could benefit from more income taxes – for instance, those countries that already have high savings and investment rates.

Question 17

QUESTION TYPE: Principle – Weaken

CONCLUSION: Governments are right to ban behavior that puts one's own health at risk.

REASONING: Hurting yourself imposes emotional and financial costs on others.

ANALYSIS: On principle questions, you just have to say "the reasoning is right" or "the reasoning is wrong". On this type of principle question, you just need to find a principle that matches the reasoning and says "we should do that" or "we should not do that".

_____

A. This is a nonsense answer. The argument never talked about endangering your ties to others. This just takes two concepts from the stimulus "harm to self" and "ties to others" and throws them together with an unrelated concept "endangering ties".

B. This *strengthens* the argument that people should not be allowed to harm themselves.

C. The argument already meets this condition. Harming yourself *does* impose financial and emotional costs on others, so we might be justified in limiting it.

D. **CORRECT.** The argument gave us just one reason for limiting harm to self: it can harm others. This answer tells us that limiting harm to others is not a good justification.

E. This talks about the moral obligations people have to each other. But the argument is about what laws the government should make.

Question 18

QUESTION TYPE: Necessary Assumption

CONCLUSION: It was wrong for Sanderson not to tell his cousin about the rumor he overheard.

REASONING: It is wrong to mislead someone, whether it's from lying or from withholding information.

ANALYSIS: This question tries to drown you in words. It states some obvious facts about lying, but uses three times the words required.

All of this is distract you from the omission the argument made. We don't know if Sanderson actually believes the plant will close! He just overheard someone say that. It's only a rumor.

If Sanderson doesn't actually think the plant will close, then he's not misleading his cousin by not from spreading the rumor.

_____

A. It doesn't matter what Sanderson thought his cousin wanted. Either way, he's still withholding information from his cousin.

B. This may seem to make Sanderson's omission have no consequences. But it's not necessary. **Negation:** Someone else told Sanderson's cousin, but Sanderson's cousin didn't believe the news. Sanderson's cousin only would have believed Sanderson.

C. **CORRECT.** If Sanderson didn't believe the factory was closing, then he had no obligation to tell his cousin false information. **Negation:** Sanderson didn't think the plant was closing.

D. This isn't necessary. The argument's point was that Sanderson's omission was as bad as lying. Whether or not Sanderson would have lied when asked, it's a fact that Sanderson omitted to pass on information.

E. This isn't necessary. Motives don't matter. The argument's point was that it's wrong to mislead, for whatever reason.

Question 19

QUESTION TYPE: Principle

PRINCIPLE: If there's a precedent:

Not contrary to basic morals → Follow precedent

If no precedent:

legal views do not contradict public opinion → judge may follow own legal views

ANALYSIS: These principle-application questions are simple. You need to take a bit of extra time on the stimulus. There are two rules:

1. Follow precedent, unless violates public morals
2. If no precedent, you can follow your own view, as long as you don't contradict public opinion

All the wrong answers will violate one or both of the rules. Go through all five answers using the first rule, and eliminate any that violate it. The only way to violate it would be: a judge not following precedent.

Then go through the remaining answers and eliminate any where the judge applies their own legal view despite opposition.

––––––––––––––

A. This violates rule two. Judges can't contradict public opinion.
B. This violates rule two. Judges can't contradict public opinion. (The public wanted 12+ tried as adults, so it violates their views to rule otherwise)
C. This violates rule one. Judges must obey precedent, as long as precedent doesn't violate moral rules. Judge Wilson failed to do that.
D. **CORRECT.** This works. There's no precedent, so rule 1 is obeyed. And there are no public views, so ruling according to the judge's legal views obeys rule 2.
E. This violates rule one. Judges must obey precedent as long as those precedents obey the moral rules of society.

Question 20

QUESTION TYPE: Most Strongly Supported

FACTS:

1. Volunteers had amusia – difficulty remembering tunes and telling melodies apart.
2. The volunteers heard shifts in pitch as big as the difference between piano keys.
3. The volunteers couldn't tell the pitches apart.
4. But the volunteers were able to track timing well.

ANALYSIS: I'm going to summarize this information further. We know three things about those who have amusia:

- They can't tell songs apart
- They can't tell pitch
- They can tell timing.

This only really supports one idea: amusia is more likely to be caused by lack of pitch judgment than lack of timing judgement. This is true because those with amusia seem to be able to track musical time!

––––––––––––––

A. There are two problems. First, we don't know if the volunteers had a *highly developed* sense of timing. We just know they could track timing – maybe everyone can do that. Second, we don't know if their latch of pitch recognition is what *caused* the volunteers to be good at timing.
B. **CORRECT.** This is well supported. We know three things: The volunteers had amusia, they suck at pitch, they're fine with timing.
C. Read the final sentence carefully. It never said the subjects could tell the pitch of the song. We have no evidence that subjects with amusia can ever discern timing.
D. This isn't supported. We do know that people with amusia can't tell melodies apart, yet their timing is fine. But perhaps someone who had no sense of timing *also* would be unable to tell melodies apart, even if they didn't have amusia.
E. We don't know why the subjects with amusia could judge timing. Maybe they learned it, sure, but it's possible they were born with it.

Question 21

QUESTION TYPE: Principle

CONCLUSION: Contemporary novels don't have much social significance.

REASONING: You can't enter into the novelist's mind in contemporary novels.

ANALYSIS: I've simplified the reasoning/conclusion to make the gap more obvious. The main gap is between the conclusion and the evidence. The conclusion says modern novels have no social significance. But nothing in the evidence says what makes a novel lack social significance.

I quickly skimmed through the answers and saw only C, D and E mentioned social significance, and only E linked social significance to evidence from the argument (e.g. getting into the mind of novelists).

There are other, smaller gaps in this argument. For instance, we don't know that sensationalism prevents you from seeing the moral perspective of characters. But that's a small gap compared to the utter lack of evidence about lack of social significance. I didn't think much about this potential gap without first checking if any of the answers addressed the major gap, social significance.

A. "Moral sensibilities of the audience" isn't in the stimulus. This is a nonsense answer that takes a few words from the stimulus and strings them together in a way that's not relevant.
B. This tells us what an author should do. That's not what we're looking for. We're trying to prove that modern novels lack social significance.
C. "Moral sensibilities of the audience" isn't mentioned in the argument. This answer can't prove anything.
D. This lets us prove when something will be socially significant. We want to prove that something *is not* socially significant. In other words, we need a necessary condition for significance, while this answer gives us a sufficient condition.
E. **CORRECT.** This links the conclusion with the evidence. Without this, we have no evidence that novels lack social significance.

Question 22

QUESTION TYPE: Flawed Reasoning

CONCLUSION: The recommendations for avoiding pathogen infection must be wrong.

REASONING: Those who follow all the recommendations are more likely to get sick.

ANALYSIS: I've seen this flaw occur a few times on recent LSATs. You should commit it to memory. The key is that the argument didn't ask *why* one group followed the instructions precisely, and the other didn't. Maybe the group that followed the instructions precisely has a higher risk: weaker immune systems, eats meat more regularly, has less sanitary meat, etc. In that case, precautions could help, even if they don't eliminate the problem.

The argument is trying to fool you into thinking this is a scientific experiment, where people are divided into two groups and we test the influence of one factor. But that's not what happened. People may be more likely to fall into the "takes precautions" group if they are at risk. Since there's no randomness in group choice, this isn't a controlled experiment.

A. The argument is only talking about infections from meat. Other foods are irrelevant.
B. It doesn't matter how many people follow the instructions. The argument was making a claim about what happens to the entire group that follows instructions. It doesn't matter if that's 1,000 people or 100,000,000.
C. This answer is trying to convince you that some diseases can't be detected, and therefore the study missed them. It's trying to contradict a premise. That almost never happens.
Also, the premise didn't say the meat instructions group had more "symptoms" of diseases. It said they have more diseases, period. We don't know how this was measured, but presumably it was accurate. (e.g. via blood tests).
D. This contradicts the stimulus. Some people followed the instructions yet still got sick.
E. **CORRECT.** This suggests that people take precautions *because* they know they may get sick. In that case it's possible the precautions help, even though they don't eliminate the problem.

Question 23

QUESTION TYPE: Parallel Reasoning

CONCLUSION: Carnegie did not publish a nonfiction book this year.

REASONING:

1. Carnegie nonfiction → ~~profit~~
2. Profit → ~~Carnegie nonfiction~~
3. Every Carnegie book earned a profit

ANALYSIS: This is a good argument. It gives us one conditional statement. Then the argument gives us a fact that combines with the contrapositive of the conditional statement. (I drew the contrapositive above as well.)

This is a bit of a subtle argument. It makes a division within Carnegie books. There are nonfiction books and other books. The argument eliminates one category (nonfiction) because they earned a profit, so clearly all books were of another type.

A. This answer is very similar. But it's not quite right. We could only conclude this:
"Every actor acted in a non-movie role last year, and they did not have major movie roles."
It is *incorrect* to conclude that none of the actors were in movies. They might have been in movies, just not in major roles. So this is a bad argument, whereas the stimulus had a good argument.

B. This doesn't make a distinction or use the contrapositive. It just gives us a conditional statement and a fact that matches the sufficient condition. It has this structure:
A → B
A is true in one particular case, therefore B is also true in that case.

C. CORRECT. This matches exactly:
1. Marketing → ~~bonus~~
2. Bonus → ~~marketing~~
3. Every systems analyst earned a bonus.
4. Therefore, every systems analyst was not in marketing.
The biggest feature is that this answer distinguishes between two types of employees: analysts and marketing. This resembles how the stimulus distinguished between non-fiction and other books.

D. This answer is a good argument, but it doesn't match the structure. Both the stimulus and the right answer made a distinction between two types (books, and employees). This answer makes no distinction, it just applies a fact to a conditional statement.
1. Business file → has done business
2. ~~has done business~~ → ~~business file~~
3. James Benson has never done business, therefore he has no business file.

E. This is just a bad argument. It's possible that Conway Flooring installs hardwood floors in other areas. Maybe they haven't installed any in Woodbridge because no customer in Woodbridge wants hardwood floors.

Question 24

QUESTION TYPE: Must be True

FACTS:

1. Unemployed artist → social justice
2. Employed artist → ~~fame~~
3. **contrapositives:** fame → unemployed → social justice
4. ~~social justice~~ → employed → ~~fame~~

ANALYSIS: This argument is a slight stretch. It incorrectly assumes that if you are an artist you are either employed or are unemployed.

In real life, we know there are other options: retired, self-employed, part time artist, hobby artist, independently wealth artist, dropped out of the labor force artist etc.

Normally, the LSAT sticks to real life. So I don't think it's valid to assume that the opposite of employed is unemployed.

However, the right answer only works if you make this assumption. And it's not that much of a stretch. So I chose the correct answer without difficulty. It's good to see subtleties, but don't tie yourself into knots and avoid an obviously correct answer because of a tiny quibble.

Using the assumption that unemployed and employed are opposites, I made two connected statements above, numbers 3 and 4. I just took the contrapositives of each statement, and negated unemployed to employed and vice versa.

A. **CORRECT.** This is statement #3 from the facts section.
B. This is totally unsupported. It doesn't match any of the statements above.
C. This incorrectly reverses #3.
D. This incorrectly reverses #3.
E. Not quite. Assuming artists are either unemployed or employed, then we could say artists are either interested in social justice or *uninterested* in fame.
   We don't know if any artists are interested in fame. We only know that *if* an artist is interested in fame, they are unemployed.

Question 25

QUESTION TYPE: Flawed Parallel Reasoning

CONCLUSION: Forster is the burglar.

REASONING: The burglar could be Schaeffer or Forster. Schaeffer has an ironclad alibi.

ANALYSIS: This argument forgets that Schaeffer and Forster aren't the only possible suspects. There might be other potential thieves that the police don't currently suspect.

So we can't say Schaeffer is the burglar unless we rule out all other possible suspects.

The structure is: There was one robber, two suspects exist, one is ruled out, the argument incorrectly concludes the remaining suspect is guilty without ruling out the possibility of other suspects.

A. This isn't strong enough. First, we only have "good reason to believe" the primate house will be built. That's not as strong as Schaeffer's "ironclad" alibi.
   Second, there's only one robber, so Schaeffer and Forster can't both be guilty. But this argument hasn't said why the zoo can't both build a primate house *and* refurbish the polar bear exhibit.
B. This is an incorrect negation. It's a different flaw.
   Statement: Lineup → Reasonable
   Incorrect Negation: ~~Lineup~~ → ~~Reasonable~~
C. This answer says what Iano *should* do. That's a moral principle. The stimulus was a question of fact: Forster *is* the robber. On the LSAT, fact and moral principle are completely different.
D. **CORRECT.** This matches the error. There are two options that are, in fact, exclusive: the company can't move to both Evansville and Rivertown. But, like the stimulus, this answer forgets there are other options. The company might decide not to move, or it might move to some other place (Smithsburg?). The argument should have excluded all other options apart from Evansville or Rivertown.
E. This is a good argument. There are only two candidates, so one of them does have to be elected. In the stimulus, the author didn't say the two suspects were the *only* two suspects.

Section IV – Logic Games
Game 1 – Radio Station
Questions 1–6

Setup

This game tests your ability to apply the rules and make deductions on the spot. There are a few very restricted points in this game. If you know the rules + these restricted points, you can do this game very, very fast. I did it in less than five minutes.

If you don't know the rules, it will be a slow, hard game. You should always try to memorize the rules before you start, and look to see what points have more restrictions than others.

For example, the first and last points are restricted. First is restricted because N always goes first. Last is restricted because S always goes last. We'll see this in the rules below.

First, we need to figure out how to draw the two news updates. I looked at the first question to see how the testmakers represented this game and I decided this was the best way:

1 __ __ __

2 __ __

Next, I read all the rules. I decided to draw the fourth rule first. We know national is always first within its group. So there are two options. National in group 1, and national in group 2:

Scenario 1

1 N __ __

2 __ __

Scenario 2

1 __ __ __   I

2 N __

On the second diagram, International must be in group 1. That's because each group needs at least one segment of local interest (rule 3), and International/National are both general. I've drawn International up and to the right in scenario 2 as a reminder of this deduction.

Drawing these two scenarios may seem like a small, obvious deduction, but it greatly simplifies the game.

Next, I drew the two remaining rules on their own. Sports is always last in its group, and *if* international and weather are in the same group, then international is before weather:

__ – S

I – W

Finally, Traffic has no rules:

It's important to pay attention to the restricted spaces. Many questions place a variable in last place; for example, question two places traffic last in the first segment.

If traffic is last in one group, then sports must be last in the other group – because sports always has to be last. This is a huge deduction, and it applies to *any* scenario where a question places someone last (that isn't sports).

This game is very open ended in the setup, but it's made in such a way that it becomes *very* restricted once one of the first or last spots is filled. Since national is always first in its group, then if someone fills the first spot in one group, you know national is first in the other group.

It's important that you memorize a few things:

- Who is general (I, N) and who is local (T, W, S)
- Who must go last: S
- Who must go first: N
- The rule about I before W

If you know these four things, the game is incredibly easy. If you struggled with it, I suspect you didn't know all four as well as you should.

Main Diagram

Scenario 1

1 N __ __ __

2 __ __ __

Scenario 2

1   I
   __ __ __

2 N __

① __ – S

② I – W

③ Ⓣ

Note: Scenario 2 has International above and to the right of group one as a reminder that International can't go in group 2. Rule 3 says each group needs at least one report of local interest. National and International are both general.

Question 1

For acceptable order questions, go through the rules and use them to eliminate answers one by one.

Rule 3 eliminates **E**. Segment two needs a report of local interest.

Rule 4 eliminates **A**. National is the longest report in its segment.

Rule 5 eliminates **C**. Sports is always the shortest segment in its group.

Rule 6 eliminates **D**. International is earlier than weather if they're in the same group.

B is **CORRECT**. It violates no rules.

Question 2

This question places the traffic report last, in the first segment. First, draw that:

1 __ __ T

2 __ __

Then, think about who must go last. S must go last. So that means S goes last in group 2:

1 __ __ T

2 __ S

Whenever you make a deduction, you should check if it's the answer. It is. **E is CORRECT.**

Question 3

This question says national is last in the second segment. That's scenario 2 from our setup:

```
            I
1  __  __  __
2  N   __
```

International has to be in group 1, because the second segment needs a report of local interest. National and International are both general.

The question is asking how many people can go first in the first group. It's best to go by elimination.

- National can't go first, because it's in the second group on this question.
- Sports also can't go first, because it's always last in its group.

That leaves: traffic, international and weather.

Weather can't go first in the first group, because weather is always after international.

So only traffic and international are left. They have no restrictions about going first, so that this point I'd be comfortable picking **B: two.**

But just to be safe, I"ll draw two scenarios that prove each can go first. If you know your rules, it should take less than ten second to draw each scenario. If you can't draw these quickly, you need to practice. Drawing rapid, correct diagrams is an essential games skill.

```
1 [T]  I   W        1 [I]  T   W
2  N   S            2  N   S
```

These two diagrams prove that both international and traffic can go first in the first segment.

So **B** is **CORRECT.**

Question 4

This question asks what CANNOT be true. You should use past scenarios to eliminate answers. Anything that worked on another question *can* be true.

A and **C** were possible on question 3. They're both in this scenario:

```
1 I   T   W
2 N   S
```

B happened in the right answer on the first question.

D is **CORRECT.** Weather can't go first in group 1. I'll explain why this can't happen. National is the other report that has to go first, so it's the restricting factor.

We're trying to place weather first in group 1, so we'd have to place national in group 2. That was scenario 2 in our setup:

```
            I
1  __  __  __
2  N   __
```

By placing national in group 2, we must place international in group 1. That's because rule 3 says every group needs a report of local interest, and N/I are both general.

So weather and international are both in group 1. And rule six says International is before weather if they're in the same group.

This answer proves **E** is possible and therefore incorrect:

```
1 T   I   S
2 N  [W]
```

Question 5

This question asks us which answer will fully determine the order of the reports.

I didn't know how to approach this question. But I looked through the answers to see which ones were harder to do.

I'll explain what I mean by harder. The rules says sports has to be last, for example. So if an answer places sports last (like **D** does) then that answer is satisfying a rule, and therefore it is easy to do.

An answer like **E** is a bit harder, because it places something last that isn't sports.

B and **C** are not hard, because they both place national first, and national has to be first.

A is hard. The rules say international is before weather. So if international is last in the first group, then weather must not be in the first group. Also, since Sports must go last, placing international last forces Sports into the second group.

So using two separate rules to measure this answer choice, **A** is hard.
(The rules are: "S last" and "I before W".)

Applying the hard/easy test, we're down to **A** and **E** to try first. Let's try **A.** I'm going to draw it step by step:

Place international last in group 1:

1 __ __ I
2 __ __

This forces Sports to be last in group 2:

1 __ __ I
2 __ S

Weather also has to be in group 2, since weather has to go after international if they're in the same group:

1 __ __ I
2 W S

National always has to go first, so national goes in group 1:

1 N __ I
2 W S

This leaves T to go second in group 1:

1 N T I
2 W S

So, **A** is **CORRECT;** placing International last in group 1 determines the entire order.

But let's make sure that **E** doesn't also fully determine everything. I do check the other plausible answer just to make sure I didn't make a mistake.

Placing weather last in the first segment does force Sports to be last in the second segment:

1 __ __ W
2 __ S

But that's all we get. We can put international, traffic and national wherever we want, as long as we put national first in the group it's in. There are no rules restricting traffic and international now that weather is last. In fact, placing weather last means that answer **E** is partly an "easy" answer to do.

If I correctly predict hard answers and think one solves the question, then I don't test the other answers. There's no need.

I already partly tested them by checking that they obeyed a rule. There's never going to be a crazy, Rube-Golberg-esque reason why obeying a rule forces everything else to fall into place.

Question 6

This question places traffic first in the first segment. You should draw that:

1 <u>T</u> __ __

2 __ __

Next, ask yourself how this affects the existing rules. In the setup, we saw that national has to be first. So if national isn't first in group 1, it must be first in group 2:

     I

1 <u>T</u> __ __

2 <u>N</u> __

I've also drawn International in group 1. We saw this in the setup, though I'll remind you again why this has to happen: rule 3 says that each segment needs a local report. National and International are both general. So they can't both go in group 1.

There's nothing else that *must* be true in this scenario. So at this point, you should stop and eliminate a few answers that contradict the diagram. Any answer that can't be true on the diagram is wrong.

The diagram contradicts **A−D**! *None* of them are possible on our diagram. This is why I always draw a diagram of what must be true – typically this eliminates all or almost all of the wrong answers.

(There's only one answer that might not seem obviously wrong: **C**. The reason weather can't go second in the first segment is because weather has to be after international. If weather is in group 1, then the order it T – I – W.)

This diagram proves that **E** is **CORRECT.**

1 <u>T</u> <u>I</u> <u>S</u>

2 <u>N</u> <u>[W]</u>

Game 2 – Five Houses
Questions 7–12

Setup

This game is unusual in that you can draw four scenarios that cover absolutely every possibility. This used to be common on older games, but I don't see it much on new games.

Typically, I don't draw more than two scenarios, because the possibilities are too open ended. But in this case, the four scenarios were very, very useful.

When I made them it was obvious the game was quite restricted, that's why I drew more than four. When I redid this game I timed myself, and with the scenarios I finished in 3 minutes 30 seconds!

Let's talk about how to draw the scenarios. You need a good grasp of the rules and how they interact.

- R is first or second.
- T is first or fifth

So if R is first, T is fifth. And if T is first, R is second. That's one major restriction. Next major rule:

- Q or V is third

Again, a major restriction. If one isn't third, the other is. Final major restriction:

- Q cannot be beside S.

This often determines whether Q or V is third.

Look over those rules to make sure you know them. Now, let's make some scenarios, using R and T as limiting factors. The first scenario has R first. The second third scenarios have R second and T fifth. The fourth scenario has T first.

Scenario 1: R first, T fifth

R	__	__	__	T
1	2	3	4	5

Next, we need to place Q, S and V. Q can't be third, because then it would be beside S no matter where S went.

So V is third, and Q/S are split between second and fourth:

		Q , S		
R	__	V	__	T
1	2	3	4	5

(Q, S comma indicates they fill the remaining slots and are reversible. I often prefer this to drawing Q/S)

Scenario 2: R second, T fifth, Q third

If R is second, there are two possibilities: T first or T fifth. This scenario is T fifth.

__	R	__	__	T
1	2	3	4	5

Next, either Q or V can be third. For this scenario, we'll put Q third

__	R	Q	__	T
1	2	3	4	5

Q and S can't be together, so this means S is first and V is fourth.

S	R	Q	V	T
1	2	3	4	5

Scenario 3: R second, T fifth, V third

If R is second, there are two possibilities: T first or T fifth. This scenario is T fifth.

	R			T
1	2	3	4	5

In scenario 2, we placed Q third. In this scenario, we'll place V third (either Q or V has to go third):

	R	V		T
1	2	3	4	5

Now Q and S are interchangeable:

Q/S	R	V	S/Q	T
1	2	3	4	5

Note: I've drawn the interchangeability differently than I did in scenario 1. For some reason, the Q/S method felt more natural here. Choose whichever method you like, they mean the same thing.

Scenario 4: R second, T first

If R is second, there are two possibilities: T first or T fifth. We already drew the two T fifth scenarios. This scenario is T first.

T	R			
1	2	3	4	5

Now we have to place Q, V and S. Q or V has to go third. We can't put V third, because then QS would be in fourth and fifth, and they can't go beside each other.

So Q is third, V is fourth and S is fifth:

T	R	Q	V	S
1	2	3	4	5

Those are all the scenarios. If any of them don't make sense, reread the rules, and try drawing them yourself. Probably you've missed one of the rules.

The key to logic games is that everything happens for a reason, and the rules are the reason. To truly understand a game you must know the rules like the back of your hand.

Mind you, it's a good idea to try building the four scenarios yourself anyway, even if you understand them. These scenarios are excellent practice for the kind of sequential deductions that are tested again and again on logic games.

Note: On the questions, I'll expect you to be aware of the four scenarios. I've listed them more close together in the main diagram section. I'll reference scenarios in the questions by number.

Main Diagram

Scenario 1

		Q , S		
R		V		T
1	2	3	4	5

Scenario 2

S	R	Q	V	T
1	2	3	4	5

Scenario 3

Q/S	R	V	S/Q	T
1	2	3	4	5

Scenario 4

T	R	Q	V	S
1	2	3	4	5

Note: draw these scenarios yourself before reading the explanations, and make sure you understand them. I'll be referencing them by number in the explanations for the questions. If you not sure how I made one of the scenarios, go back to the setup section.

Question 7

Unusually, this first question is not an "acceptable order" question. Whenever that happens, it's a strong sign you were supposed to make upfront deductions.

Quarry can be fourth in scenarios 1 and 3. Here they are:

Scenario 1

$$\begin{array}{ccccc} & & Q,S & & \\ \underline{R} & \underline{} & \underline{V} & \underline{} & \underline{T} \\ 1 & 2 & 3 & 4 & 5 \end{array}$$

Scenario 3

$$\begin{array}{ccccc} \underline{Q/S} & \underline{R} & \underline{V} & \underline{S/Q} & \underline{T} \\ 1 & 2 & 3 & 4 & 5 \end{array}$$

You can use these scenarios to eliminate answers. Any answer that doesn't have to be true in both scenarios is wrong.

Scenario 3 eliminates **A, C** and **D.**

Scenario 1 eliminates **B.**

E is CORRECT.

Question 8

This question asks what answer fully determines the order. I used the scenarios to eliminate answers. For example, **A** asks whether placing Quarry third determines everything.

Q can be third in both scenarios 2 and 4. So clearly, placing Q third doesn't determine everything, as those two scenarios are different. **A** is not right.

B is also wrong. R is first in the first scenario, yet there are two possibilities: Q and S are interchangeable between second and first:

Scenario 1

$$\begin{array}{ccccc} & & Q,S & & \\ \underline{R} & \underline{} & \underline{V} & \underline{} & \underline{T} \\ 1 & 2 & 3 & 4 & 5 \end{array}$$

C is **CORRECT.** S can be second only in the first scenario. And if S is second, Q is fourth, so everything else is determined:

$$\begin{array}{ccccc} \underline{R} & \boxed{S} & \underline{V} & \underline{Q} & \underline{T} \\ 1 & 2 & 3 & 4 & 5 \end{array}$$

D is wrong. T can be fifth in the 1st, 2nd and 3rd scenarios.

E is wrong. V can be fourth in both the 2nd and 4th scenarios.

Remember, an answer is wrong if there are multiple possibilities. That means the placement in the answer doesn't completely determine the order.

Question 9

This question says S is earlier than Q. You should check what scenarios this is possible in. Scenarios 1, 2 and 3 allow S to be earlier than Q:

Scenario 1

	Q , S			
R		V		T
1	2	3	4	5

Scenario 2

S	R	Q	V	T
1	2	3	4	5

Scenario 3

Q/S	R	V	S/Q	T
1	2	3	4	5

This question says S is before Q. So really the three scenarios look like this:

Scenario 1

R	S	V	Q	T
1	2	3	4	5

Scenario 2

S	R	Q	V	T
1	2	3	4	5

Scenario 3

S	R	V	Q	T
1	2	3	4	5

Now you're looking for what must be true in all scenarios. Let's eliminate answers.

Scenario 2 disproves **A.** Q isn't fourth in that scenario.

Scenario 1 disproves **B.** R is not second in that scenario.

Scenario 1 disproves **C.** S is not first in that scenario.

D is CORRECT. T must be last in all three scenarios.

Scenario 2 disproves **E.** V is fourth in that scenario.

Question 10

This is a could be true question. One answer will be possible in at least one scenario. The other four answers will be *impossible* in all four scenarios.

A is **CORRECT.** Q can be first in scenario 3:

Q	R	V	S	T
1	2	3	4	5

B-E are impossible in all scenarios. If you look at the four scenarios, it's clearly impossible to do any of the last four answers. I'll give a bit more detail though. I'll expect you to know the rules to follow how I'm making deduction on these answers.

B: Placing Q fifth forces T first, and R second (rules 1 and 3). V has to go third because V or Q goes third. That leaves S to go fourth, beside Q, which isn't allowed (rule 4).

C: If V is first, R is second and T if fifth (rules 1 and 2). Q has to go third because one of V/Q goes third. That leaves S to go fourth, beside Q, which isn't allowed (rule 4).

D: If V is second, Q is third (rule 3) and R is 1 (rule 1). This forces T fifth (rule 2). That leave S to go third, beside Q, which isn't allowed (rule 4).

E: If V is fifth, T is first (rule 2). That makes R second (rule 1). Q is third (rule 3). That leaves S to go fourth, beside Q, which isn't allowed (rule 4).

If you're not clear on any of these answers, review the four scenarios from the main diagram section, and reread the rules. Then try to draw the answer yourself. These answers are excellent practice for the kind of sequential deductions that logic games ask you to make.

Question 11

This question asks what must be true if V is third. V is third only in scenarios 1 and 3. We're looking for something that must be true, so you need to find something that doesn't change.

R, Q and S can all change places between the two scenarios. Only T doesn't change: it's always fifth.

E is **CORRECT.**

Question 12

Rule substitution questions are harder than other questions, but they're not as hard as you think. The key is to eliminate silly answers. Remember, four of the answers are *wrong*. You don't have to give them any respect. They're mostly stupid answers. Your goal should be to prove they're stupid.

An answer can be wrong for two reasons on a rule substitution question:

1. It allows something not allowed under the normal rules.
2. It restricts something allowed under the normal rules.

I go through each answer and try to disprove it, applying those tests. If an answer seems plausible and doesn't violate either test, then I keep it as a contender. Once I've eliminated some answers, I can test the remaining answers more thoroughly.

A isn't restrictive enough. It only blocks R from being fourth, and therefore it allows this scenario:

T	Q	V	S	R
1	2	3	4	5

(It's wrong, because R can't be fifth normally.)

B seems plausible. Let's skip it.

C describes something that has to be true (V *is* always 3rd or 4th), but that's not what we're looking for. We want a rule that matches the effects of the original rule, but this new rule allows this possibility:

T	Q	V	S	R
1	2	3	4	5

V is third (like the rule says), but R is fifth, which isn't allowed.

D isn't true. In the 1st scenario, Q doesn't have to be beside R: Q can be fourth. So this answers prevents possibilities that are normally allowed.

E allows possibilities that normally aren't allowed, like this:

S	V	Q	R	T
1	2	3	4	5

T is shown fifth, so the rule in **E** is obeyed. But R is no longer 1st or 2nd.

So let's look at **B** again. It says that R must be earlier than V. If you look over all four scenarios, you'll see that V can only be 3rd or 4th.

If V is 3rd, then R must be 1st or 2nd. This obeys the old rule.

If V is fourth, the Q must be 3rd, since Q or V always has to be third (rule 3). So this means that once again R must be 1st or 2nd to be earlier than V.

Therefore, the rule is replaced either way. **B** is **CORRECT.**

Game 3 – Sunken Artifacts
Questions 13–18

Setup

This is a rules based game. If you know the rules like the back of your hand, this game is easy. If you struggle to remember the rules, this game is hard.

The key to most modern games is to slow down on the setup, and memorize the rules. If you know all the rules, you'll go *much* faster through the questions.

There are three groups in this game: Iceland, Norway and Sweden. The first question shows you the best way to set them up:

```
I

N

S
```

These are three vertical groups. There are no lines beside them for artifacts, because it's possible for a country to have *no* artifacts.

I drew the third rule first. We need more artifacts in Iceland than Norway:

```
  ⸜ I  —
>⸝
    N

    S
```

The arrow and the "greater-than" sign are an improvised reminder of this. Note that now we also need at least one artifact in Iceland, so I've drawn a line there for that artifact.

I then drew the second rule directly on the diagram. X is from Norway or Sweden. I put this in two scenarios:

```
  ⸜ I  —  —
>⸝
    N  X
       ―
    S
```

```
  ⸜ I  —
>⸝
    N

    S  X
       ―
```

In the first scenario, Iceland must have at least two artifacts, due to rule 3.

Note that Norway can have at most two artifacts (in either scenario), in which case Iceland would have three.

Often, drawing dual scenarios leads to extra deductions. In this game, there were no new deductions. However, I do find the dual scenarios are useful for a few reasons:

- They serve as a reminder of the rule about X's origin.
- They make it easier to visualize possibilities while looking at them.
- They remove one rule from the list of rules.

I find removing one rule from the list of rules significantly simplifies the game. The more rules you have directly on the diagram, the easier it is to remember the remaining rules.

Next, there are two rules that can't be added to the diagram. WY must be together, and if V is in Iceland, then Z is in Sweden:

$$V_I \rightarrow Z_S$$

If you *ever* make a mistake with contrapositives, you should also draw the contrapositive of the rule:

$$\cancel{Z}_S \rightarrow \cancel{V}_I$$

However, once you master contrapositives at an intuitive level, you no longer need to draw them.

There's no major deductions on this setup. So you should memorize the rules before moving on, as the game is going to test you on your mastery of the rules.

Main Diagram

>$\big($ I — —
　N　X
　S

>$\big($ I —
　N
　S　X

① WY

② $V_I \rightarrow Z_S$

　$\cancel{Z}_S \rightarrow \cancel{V}_I$

Question 13

For acceptable order questions, go through the rules and use them to eliminate answers one by one.

Rule 1 eliminates **A**. W and Y must come from the same country.

Rule 2 eliminates **E**. X has to come from Norway or Sweden.

Rule 3 eliminates **C**. Iceland needs to have more articles than Norway.

Rule 4 eliminates **D**. If Iceland has V, then Sweden must have Z.

B is **CORRECT**. It violates no rules.

Question 14

First, you should draw the local rule. Y and Z originated in Iceland. Actually, this means that WYZ came from Iceland, because WY are always together:

$$> \big(\; \begin{array}{c} I \\ N \\ S \end{array} \; \underline{W} \;\; \underline{Y} \;\; \underline{Z}$$

The question is asking for the minimum number of artifacts that come from Sweden. Let's see if we can do zero. VX are the remaining artifacts. Can we put them both in Norway?:

$$> \big(\; \begin{array}{c} I \\ N \\ S \end{array} \; \begin{array}{ccc} \underline{W} & \underline{Y} & \underline{Z} \\ \underline{V} & \underline{X} & \end{array}$$

There's nothing wrong with doing this. It violates no rules. So it's possible zero artifacts originated in Sweden. **A is CORRECT.**

Remember, if a diagram doesn't violate any rules, it's allowed.

Question 15

This question asks what cannot be true. You want to look for answers that are hard to do. By "hard" I mean answers that make it harder to obey a rule. "Easy" answers are those that obey a rule.

For instance, **A** is hard because it places two artifacts in Norway (meaning we'd need three in Iceland) but easy because it places X in Norway (obeying rule 2).

B and **C** are easy because they place at least two artifacts in Iceland. That helps obey rule 3 (Iceland has more than Norway).

D makes things easy because it meets the necessary condition of rule 4. Since Z originated in Sweden, it now doesn't matter where V goes.

E is places two artifacts in Norway. This means we'd need three in Iceland (rule 3). That's hard. **E** also *doesn't* place X in Norway. So to obey rule 2 we'd have to put X in Sweden.

That means only Z and V are left to go in Iceland. So we don't have enough to put more in Iceland than Norway, and **E** is **CORRECT.** (Actually, it's not even possible to put both Z and V in Iceland, due to rule 4).

So there should be a method to your madness on CANNOT be true questions. Ask if an answer obeys a rule (easy) or makes a rule harder to obey.

I said **A** was hard too, so let's disprove it. It's true that **A** puts two artifacts in Norway. But it's definitely possible to put the remaining three artifacts in Iceland. Matter of fact, we saw this diagram in question 14:

$$> \big(\; \begin{array}{c} I \\ N \\ S \end{array} \; \begin{array}{ccc} \underline{W} & \underline{Y} & \underline{Z} \\ \underline{V} & \underline{X} & \end{array}$$

When I did this question on timed conditions I followed the exact same process. I kept A, I fast-eliminated B, C and D, and then I saw E was hard so I tried it. E worked, then I eliminated A to make sure. Didn't take long because I didn't pay much attention to the answers that seemed easy.

Question 16

This question says that W and X originated in Sweden. Actually, this means that WYX originated in Sweden, since W and Y always go together:

I

N

S W Y X
    — — —

The next most restrictive rule is that Iceland must have more than Norway. And there are only two artifacts left to place.

If we place one artifact in Iceland and one in Norway, they'll each have an *equal* number of artifacts.

So we can't put any artifacts in Norway. We have to put either V or Z in Iceland, and the other will go in Sweden.

> I Z/V
     —
 N

   S W Y X V/Z
     — — — —

(V and Z can't both go in Iceland because of rule 4)

A is CORRECT.

Question 17

I looked at past questions to answer this. This diagram from question 14 proves that V and X can originate in Norway:

> I W Y Z
     — — —
 N V X
   — —

  S

The right answer to question 15 shows that neither W nor Y can originate in Norway.

This is because WY always go together. That means there are two in Norway, so we'd need three in Iceland. But X has to go in Norway or Sweden, so there *aren't* three artifacts to originate in Iceland if WY are in Norway.

If that didn't make sense, look carefully at the rules and try to draw WY in Norway without violating a rule. You can't.

Only Z is left. Can Z go in Norway? This diagram proves that it can:

> I W Y
     — —
 N Z
   —

  S X V
    — —

C is CORRECT. X, Y and Z can go in Norway.

Question 18

On question 15, I talked about using a hard/easy test to judge which answers to try first on CANNOT be true questions.

"Hard" is an answer that doesn't work with a rule and makes it harder to obey a rule. "Easy" is an answer that conforms with a rule.

For instance, putting V in Iceland is "hard". That's because it restricts the game by forcing Z into Sweden. So *not* putting V with Iceland is "easy" because it removes a potential restriction.

Therefore **A** is easy. We should skip it and try other answers.

B and **C** are a mix. **B** does remove the fourth rule (because V isn't in Iceland). And C does place WY together.

But on the other hand, both answers force X to be in Norway, because X isn't in Sweden (rule 2), and they both take up two artifacts, so that makes it harder to put more artifacts in Iceland than Norway. We should try both answers.

D is easy. It complies with rule 2 (X in Norway or Sweden) and with rule 4 (Z is in Sweden, so now it doesn't matter where V goes).

E seems hard because it has four artifacts in Sweden, but there's nothing wrong with it. We can just put Z in Iceland:

```
   I   Z
>(
   N

   S   V   W   X   Y
```

This obeys all the rules. So let's try **B** and **C**.

This diagram shows **B** is possible:

```
   I   W   Y
>(
   N   X

   S   V   Z
```

C is **CORRECT.** If only WY are in Sweden, X must go in Norway:

```
   I   __  __
>(
   N   X

   S   W   Y
```

Now, we need to place more artifacts in Iceland than in Norway (rule 3). Only V and Z are left. But they can't both go in Iceland, because of rule 4. If V is in Iceland, Z goes to Sweden. So **C** is impossible.

Note: it took a lot of writing to judge whether all five answers were "easy" or "hard". But that's because it takes a lot of words to explain things out loud. If you know the rules, you can see these answers as hard/easy almost instantly.

It's that process I'd like you to try to practice. Ask if answers conform with a rule, or make it harder to obey a rule.

Game 4 – Summit Workpieces
Questions 19–23

Setup

This is an unusual game. I've never seen one quite like this.

However, the *principles* underlying this game are not different from other logic games. I was able to finish it quite quickly.

If you had trouble with this game, I recommend two steps:

1. Try some older games. They're different, but the principles are similar. That means they're good practice for testing your ability to handle unfamiliar games.
2. Repeat games. You want an intuition for the patterns in games. That's what will let you solve unique games like this.

What are the principles underlying this game? Two main ones:

- Knowing the rules.
- Seeing the most restricted point.

The most restricted point is J. L and K can't transfer to J. So only M can, and therefore M *must* transfer to J every turn.

It turns out the four rounds don't matter. This game is all about seeing what's possible within a single round.

Here's the diagram I made. I did draw the four rounds, but they're not important.

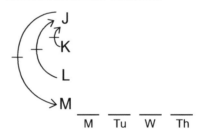

Here's the main diagram with the rules added. The arrows with a cross indicate a transfer is impossible between those two variables:

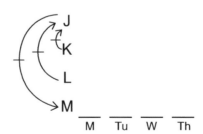

I just looked at this diagram for every question. There's not really much more to this game, as long as you notice that M has to transfer to J every round.

Main Diagram

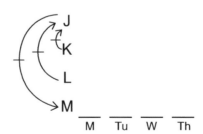

76

Question 19

For acceptable order questions, go through the rules and use them to eliminate answers one by one.

Rule 1 eliminates **E.** J can't transfer to M

Rule 2 eliminates **D.** K can't transfer to J.

Rule 3 eliminates **C.** L can't transfer to J.

You have to do a *bit* of work to choose between **A** and **B.** Everyone needs to send and receive a transfer.

I went through both answers and looked at who received. I saw that in **B,** K receives twice. That can't happen.

Therefore, **A** is **CORRECT.** It violates no rules.

Question 20

This question tests a deduction you can make in the setup. Look at the arrows from the main diagram:

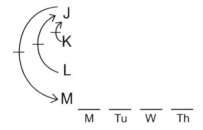

Both K and L can't transfer to J. So only M can transfer to J. And since J has to receive something, M has to transfer to J every workday after Monday.

E is **CORRECT.**

Question 21

This question asks which two employees can share a workpiece during the whole week. Basically, they'll have to pass it back and forth, without giving it to anyone else.

First, you can eliminate **D** and **E.** M can only pass to J (we saw this on question 20).

Next, you can eliminate **A** and **B.** Both K and L can't pass to J. So it's impossible for J and K/L to pass a workpiece back and force without involving a third employee.

Therefore, **C** is **CORRECT.** K and L have no restrictions about passing a workpiece between the two of them.

Question 22

This question asks what must be true if L works on the same piece on Tuesday and Thursday.

That means that L passes the workpiece to someone else on Wednesday, and that person passes it back to L for Thursday.

First of all, you can eliminate **A, B** and **C.** It doesn't matter what happens on Monday. It only matters who has L's workpiece on Wednesday, between Tuesday and Thursday. The first day order *does not* matter on this game.

Now, we have to choose between **D** and **E.** Fortunately, **D** is impossible. L can't pass it to J; that's rule 3.

E is **CORRECT.** Note that this is basically the same question as 21. Only K and L can pass a piece between the two of them. And that's what is happening on this question. L passes to K, who passes back to L. No other two people can do that.

Question 23

This was the hardest question, I found. It was the only one where I found drawings useful (besides the main drawing).

This question asks about Tuesday, but the day doesn't matter. This would be the exact same question if it was talking about any other day with transfer. On this game the days are just a distraction.

First, you can eliminate a couple answers. **C** is wrong because J can't transfer to M (rule 1).

D is wrong because K and L pass back and forth between them. This leaves J and M to transfer between each other. But J can't transfer to M (rule 1), so this doesn't work.

For the other three answers, I had to make drawings of what was happening. **Note that** M *always* transfers to J (we saw this in question 20) so I drew that as well.

I'll repeat that last line because it's important. M always has to transfer to J. We saw this in the setup. So all the drawings include this transfer.

Note also that everyone must send and receive a transfer. Two answers are wrong because they leave one employee without a transfer partner.

A has transfers from J to K, K to M, and M to J:

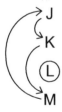

This left L without anyone to transfer with.

B has transfers from J to L, L to M and M to J:

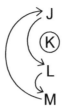

This leaves K without anyone to transfer with.

E is **CORRECT.** It has transfers from K to L and L to M. There's also the routine transfer from M to J:

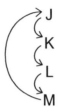

Finally, I drew a transfer from J to K, because J hadn't transferred and K hadn't received. That was just to prove to myself that this answer allowed all four people to make and receive transfer.

So **E** doesn't violate any rules and it has everyone making a transfer and everyone receiving a transfer.

Appendix: LR Questions By Type

Strengthen

Section II, #3
Section II, #7
Section II, #23
Section II, #25
Section III, #6
Section III, #8
Section III, #12

Weaken

Section II, #2
Section II, #10
Section III, #2
Section III, #10

Sufficient Assumption

Section II, #8

Parallel Reasoning

Section II, #26
Section III, #23

Flawed Parallel Reasoning

Section II, #22
Section III, #25

Necessary Assumption

Section II, #12
Section II, #15
Section II, #21
Section III, #4
Section III, #18

Must Be True

Section II, #24
Section III, #24

Most Strongly Supported

Section II, #17
Section III, #20

Paradox

Section II, #9
Section II, #11
Section III, #1
Section III, #5

Principle

Section II, #1
Section II, #6
Section III, #13
Section III, #17
Section III, #19
Section III, #21

Identify The Conclusion

Section II, #4
Section III, #3
Section III, #9

Thank You

First of all, thank you for buying this book. Writing these explanations has been the most satisfying work I have ever done. I sincerely hope they'll have been helpful to you, and I wish you success on the LSAT and as a lawyer.

If you left an Amazon review, you get an extra special thank you! I truly appreciate it. You're helping others discover LSAT Hacks.

Thanks also to Anu Panil, who drew the diagrams for the logic games. Anu, thank you for making sense of the scribbles and scans I sent you. You are surely ready to master logic games after all the work you did.

Thanks to Alison Rayner, who helped me with the layout and designed the cover. If this book looks nice, she deserves credit. Alison caught many mistakes I would never have found by myself (any that remain are my own, of course).

Thanks to Ludovic Glorieux, who put up with me constantly asking him if a design change looked good or bad.

Finally, thanks to my parents, who remained broadly supportive despite me being crazy enough to leave law school to teach the LSAT. I love you guys.

About The Author

Graeme Blake lives in Montreal Canada. He first took the LSAT in June 2007, and scored a 177. It was love at first sight. He taught the LSAT for Testmasters for a couple of years before going to the University of Toronto for law school.

Upon discovering that law was not for him, Graeme began working as an independent LSAT tutor. He teaches LSAT courses in Montreal for Ivy Global and tutors students from all around the world using Skype.

He publishes a series of LSAT guides and explanations under the title LSAT Hacks. Versions of these explanations can be found at LSAT Blog, Cambridge LSAT and LSAT Hacks, as well as amazon.com.

Graeme is also the moderator of www.reddit.com/r/LSAT, Reddit's LSAT forum. He worked for a time with 7Sage LSAT.

Graeme finds it unusual to write in the third person to describe himself, but he recognizes the importance of upholding publishing traditions. He wonders if many people read about the author pages.

You can find him at www.lsathacks.com and www.reddit.com/r/LSAT.

Graeme encourages you to get in touch by email, his address is graeme@lsathacks.com. Or you can call 514-612-1526. He's happy to hear feedback or give advice.

Further Reading

I hope you liked this book. If you did, I'd be very grateful if you took two minutes to review it on amazon. People judge a book by its reviews, and if you review this book you'll help other LSAT students discover it.

Ok, so you've written a review and want to know what to do next.

The most important LSAT books are the preptests themselves. Many students think they have to read every strategy guide under the sun, but you'll learn the most simply from doing real LSAT questions and analyzing your mistakes.

At the time of writing, there are 72 official LSATs. The most recent ones are best, but if you've got a while to study I recommend doing every test from 19 or from 29 onwards.

This series (LSAT Hacks) is a bit different from other LSAT prep books. This book is not a strategy guide.

Instead, my goal is to let you do what my own students get to do when they take lessons with me: review their work with the help of an expert.

These explanations show you a better way to approach questions, and exactly why answers are right or wrong.

If you found this book useful, here's the list of other books in the series:

(Note – the series was formerly titled "Hacking the LSAT" so the older books still have that title until I update them)

- Hacking The LSAT: Full Explanations For LSATs 29-38, Volume I
- Hacking The LSAT: Full Explanations For LSATs 29-38, Volume II
- LSAT 62 Explanations (Hacking The LSAT Series)
- LSAT 63 Explanations (Hacking The LSAT Series)
- LSAT 64 Explanations (Hacking The LSAT Series)
- LSAT 65 Explanations (Hacking The LSAT Series)
- LSAT 66 Explanations (Hacking The LSAT Series)
- LSAT 67 Explanations (Hacking The LSAT Series)
- LSAT 68 Explanations (Hacking The LSAT Series)
- LSAT 69 Explanations (Hacking The LSAT Series)
- LSAT 70 Explanations (Hacking The LSAT Series)
- LSAT 71 Explanations (Hacking The LSAT Series)
- LSAT 72 Explanations (LSAT Hacks Series)

Keep an eye out, as I'll be steadily publishing explanations for other LSATs.

If you *are* looking for strategy guides, try Manhattan LSAT or Powerscore. Unlike other companies, they use real LSAT questions in their books.

I've written a longer piece on LSAT books on Reddit. It includes links to the best LSAT books and preptests. If you're serious about the LSAT and want the best materials, I strongly recommend you read it:

http://redd.it/uf4uh

(this is a shortlink that takes you to the correct page)

Free LSAT Email Course

This book is just the beginning. It teaches you how to solve individual questions, but it's not designed to give you overall strategies for each section.

There's so much to learn about the LSAT. As a start, I've made a free, five day email course. Each day I'll send you an email teaching you what I know about a subject.

LSAT Email Course Overview

- Intro to the LSAT
- Logical Reasoning
- Logic Games
- Reading Comprehension
- How to study

What people say about the free LSAT course

These have been awesome. More please!!! - **Cailie**

Your emails are tremendously helpful. - **Matt**

Thanks for the tips! They were very helpful, and even make you feel like you studied a bit. Great insight and would love more! - **Haj**

Sign up for the free LSAT email course here

http://lsathacks.com/email-course/

p.s. I've had people say this free email course is more useful than an entire Kaplan course they took. It's 100% free. Good luck - Graeme

Made in the USA
Lexington, KY
14 August 2014